This book is to be returned on or before the last date below.
You may renew the book unless it is requested by another borrower.
THANK YOU FOR USING YOUR LIBRARY

Behind the Rainbow

THE
TRAGIC
LIFE
OF
EVA CASSIDY

Behind the Rainbow

THE
TRAGIC
LIFE
OF **EVA
CASSIDY**

JOHAN BAKKER

OMNIBUS PRESS

London / New York / Paris / Sydney / Copenhagen / Berlin / Madrid / Tokyo

Contents

Contents

Acknowledgements

Returning home from my holidays in 2001 I found an envelope on the doormat containing a CD and a letter requesting I review it. Looking at *Songbird*'s brown cover design framing a photograph that was unintentionally out of focus, my expectations were far from high. But as soon as Eva Cassidy started to sing the opening lines of 'Fields Of Gold' I was nailed to the ground. This unknown singer enchanted me for 45 minutes until the closing notes of the final song 'Over The Rainbow'. The letter told me that Eva had died at the tragically young age of 33. Listening to the album a second time it was not only Eva's voice that struck me, but her song selection as well. All possible scepticism disappeared immediately when I heard Eva sing: 'I'm going there to meet my Father, in that bright land of which I go'. Her interpretation of the lines: 'The dreams that you dared to dream really do come true' convince the listener of the fact that Eva believed them. I wanted to know more about this remarkable woman. Ten years later my fascination for Eva is still growing and has resulted in this biography.

Many people helped me during my research into the life, art and music of Eva Cassidy. I'd like to thank Dan Cassidy for visiting me at my home in Rotterdam and for telling all he could about his beloved sister; Chris Biondo for his patience and answering a seemingly endless list of emails and phone calls; Chris Charlesworth and Lucy Beevor for their editing and knowledge of musical history; Raice McLeod, Keith Grimes, Lenny

Williams, Hugh & Barbara Cassidy, Celia Murphy, Ruth Murphy, Ned Judy, Larry Melton and Eileen White for their hospitality during my trip to Maryland; Bill Straw, Chuck Brown, Anna Karen Kristinsdóttir, Jackie Fletcher, Tony Bramwell, Margret Cassidy Robinson, Henrik Thiil Nielsen, Brian Langtry, Laura Bligh, Niki Lee and Linda Olson Peebles for their clarifying views on Eva's life story; Maria van Ginneken, Laura Bol and Marente de Moor for polishing my writing; and Vincent van de Kerk and Petra Sytsma van der Ploeg for reviewing Eva's artwork. Rommy, Deborah & Sybren Bakker for believing in this project from the start and their eternal help. Thank you all!

Johan Bakker, Rotterdam, August 2011

Sources

This biography is based on personal interviews with: Dan Cassidy, Chris Biondo, Raice McLeod, Keith Grimes, Lenny Williams, Bill Straw, Hugh & Barbara Cassidy, Celia Murphy, Ruth Murphy, Chuck Brown, Anna Karen Kristinsdóttir, Jackie Fletcher, Ned Judy, Larry Melton, Tony Bramwell, Margret Cassidy Robinson, Katie Melua, Eileen White, Henrik Thiil Nielsen, Vincent van de Kerk, Brian Langtry, Laura Bligh, Niki Lee & Linda Olson Peebles

Other sources and bibliography

Anon. http://heatherw.com, April 11 2002, 'Blix Street Records Presents Kwan With Gold Record'

Cassidy, Clara. *Mother Earth News*, 1978 'Preserve Your Memories Oriental Style'

Cooper, William. www.allmusic.com, September 2000, Review 'No Boundaries'

Dalphonse, Sherri. *Washingtonian* online, May 2002, 'Songbird'

Harrington, Richard. *The Washington Post*, November. 17, 1996 'Echoes of a Voice Stilled Too Early'

Morley, Jefferson. *The Washington Post*, March 8, 1998 'When Chuck Met Eva'

Siegel, Joel E. Liner Notes *Eva By Heart* (Liaison Records, 1997)

Ward, Alex. *New York Times*, August 12, 2002. 'In Death, A Shy Singer Finally Grabs The Spotlight',

Wartofsky, Alona. *Washington City Paper*, November 20, 1992 'Side by Side'

The *Independent*, Aug 16, 2002. Review 'Imagine' by Andy Gill

Songbird: Her Story By Those Who Knew Her – Rob Burley, Jonathan Maitland and Elana Rhodes Byrd – Gotham Books, USA, 2003

Svenska Dagbladet, August 18th, 2003 Interview Chris Biondo by Harry Amster

Billboard Magazine, March 27, 2004 'Blix Street Sues Eva Cassidy Parents' by Chris Morris

Entertainment Law Reporter, October 2004

The Color Purple, novel, Harcourt Brace Jovanovich, USA, 1982 by Alice Walker

The Color Purple, Warner Brothers Video 1986, directed by Steven Spielberg

Liner notes 'Anywhere But Here' May 2004, by Michael Ingram

The Eva Cassidy Story: Over The Rainbow. Booklet musical by Theatremaster Ltd, 2005

GardeNews newsletter, by the Behnke Nurseries, Holiday 2005 issue. 'Memories of Eva Cassidy' by Larry Hurley.

Hugh Cassidy, et al. v. David Lourim, et al. United States district court for the district of Maryland. March 6, 2008.

Washington City Paper. June 4, 2008 'Selling Eva Cassidy By The Pound' by Dave McKenna

Sunday Express, March 28, 2010 'Will Kate Winslet Play Songbird Eva Cassidy?'

The Wall Street Journal, September 29, 2010 'The Godfather of Go-Go' by Jim Fusilli

Eva Cassidy forum Yahoo group

www.evacassidy.org (website about Eva Cassidy's life and music by her cousin Laura Bligh. Info about the albums *Eva By Heart*, *Time After Time*, *Imagine*, *American Tune*, *Somewhere* and interviews with Mike Dove, Al Dale, David Christopher and Eileen White)

www.evacassidy.dk (EvaSongs, website about Eva's songs by Henrik Thiil Nielsen and Torbjörn Skobe)

www.evacassidy.com (website about Eva's artwork by her sisters Margret and Anette)

www.oaksite.co.uk

www.cassidyclan.org

Chapter 1

Made In Germany

"I was made in Germany," Eva Cassidy used to tell her friends. It was a joke, of course, but any journey to the heart and soul of Eva Cassidy must begin in central Europe for it was there, in the Rhineland, where she was conceived and where her heart started to beat after her mother, Barbara, became pregnant for the third time.

Let's follow the Rhine upstream to the beginnings of this beautiful but tragic story. The German mountains of the Eifel, Westerwald, Hunsrück and Taunus rise majestically on both banks of the river, dotted with forests, small castles, little white churches and quaint brick houses. The great river bends sharply at St Goarshausen, where the mountains reach more than 100 metres high. This narrow part of the Rhine can be dangerous for river traffic; a barge carrying 2,400 tonnes of sulphuric acid capsized here in January 2011. The highest rock on the eastern bank is called the Loreley after the mermaid who lured fishermen to their deaths by singing the most beautiful songs they had ever heard. Can there be any better instance of the mythic power of the female voice?

In Bingen the Rhine branches off into the much smaller Nahe river. A few miles to the west lies Bad Kreuznach, a medium-sized spa town with thermal baths and a quaint town square. The main retail street,

Wilhelmstrasse, ends at an old bridge across the Nahe which is lined with medieval houses. Faust, the local chemists, is named after Goethe's famous alchemist who sold his soul to the devil. The German counterpart of blues singer and guitarist Robert Johnson was born in this town. Eva Cassidy's grandfather and great-grandfather both had furniture workshops in the town centre. The final mile to Ledderhoserweg, the street where Eva's grandfather Karl built the small cream-coloured house at number 11 on landfill in the thirties, is steep. His wife, Wilhelmina, gave birth to two daughters in this house: Eva's mother, Barbara, in 1939 and Katrin in 1944.

Eva's great-grandfather, Hermann Krätzer, grew up in Saksen, where his predecessors had lived for centuries. The family still has an old photograph of him as an apprentice window maker, wearing an apron and working with glass. As a young man he liked to travel, and during one of his journeys to the Rhineland he arrived at the point where the Rhine branches off into the Nahe. He took one look at the valley and decided to settle there.

In his new hometown of Bad Kreuznach he met his future wife, Maria. She gave birth to two sons: Karl and Hermann Junior. During the First World War Hermann Senior had to leave his furniture shop for active duty, eventually becoming a personal bodyguard to Kaiser Wilhelm II, who had taken up residence in the Bad Kreuznach sanatorium from 1917. It was used by the general staff until extreme flooding in January 1918 led them to relocate to a spa in Belgium. Hermann Senior came to an unfortunate end on a battlefield in Poland in the last year of the war, killed by a bayonet.

His two sons both became cabinet makers. Young Hermann produced splendid tables and chairs, but Karl was marginally the better craftsman and made solid yet beautiful furniture, working with wood as an artist works with paint. He also enjoyed classical music, especially the work of 19th-century German composers like Brahms and Beethoven and, like his father, he liked to travel and studied geography. In the early thirties, Karl predicted that a second world war was coming, which at the time was greeted with much mockery from the townspeople.

As fascism strengthened its grip on Germany, Bad Kreuznach became a centre of opposition to the Nazi regime. Hugo Salzmann, an infamous communist and anti-fascist, coordinated resistance against the Hitler movement from here. Miraculously, he survived the war, later representing the Communist Party in the Bad Kreuznach city council in 1945.

Eva's grandfather, Karl, had more sympathy for the communists in his town than for the Nazis and joined Salzmann's cause. He was caught with communist pamphlets in his possession in 1933 and sent to jail for six months. On release he helped several townsfolk to escape the horrors of impending war but was unable to avoid having to fulfill his own duty and was sent to fight in Poland, far away from his home.

Because of his political stance, Karl managed to survive by doing the bare minimum for his superiors though he was several times interned in a military prison. In the final year of the war, as he was making his usual rounds with a superior officer, the officer asked him to look after his bicycle while he disappeared into a shop to buy cigarettes. Karl didn't give it a second thought. He jumped on the bike and escaped, leaving the officer behind. He cycled all the way from Poland to Bad Kreuznach, taking an enormous detour via Switzerland, to be reunited with his wife, Wilhelmina, and his daughters, Barbara and Katrin.

He came home to a town transformed by war. Bad Kreuznach's Jewish citizens had been deported to Theresienstadt concentration camp in Sudetenland and the neighbourhood had been the target of Allied bombs, which had destroyed the Wehrmacht barracks in Bosenheimer Strasse, Alzeyer Strasse and Franziska-Puricelli Strasse and the important Berlin to Paris railway that passed through the town.

Lieutenant Colonel John Kaup, the last commander of Bad Kreuznach, prevented further destruction in the town by offering no resistance to the advancing American regiments. It was captured by the Americans on March 16, 1945 and became part of the Allied French occupation zone. Shortly before the Allies took control of the town, retreating German troops blew up part of the old bridge over the Nahe and destroyed the bridgeheads, making it difficult for the town's inhabitants to obtain food supplies. Several acquaintances of the Krätzers did not survive the war.

3

Eva's grandparents are not buried in the cemetery at the Mittlerer Flurweg: Karl and Wilhelmina donated their bodies to medical science after their deaths. A generous spirit of idealism, which Eva certainly inherited, runs in the family.

Karl's first daughter, Barbara, was born in 1939. She was a sensitive child who at the age of four never understood the reason for war and was still stupefied by it when she reached 70. Barbara continues to feel the impact of this harrowing period in history. She lived through the worst of it and was constantly exposed to suffering: the bombings, the ruined houses, the food shortages, the sad letters that arrived from the Front reporting missing or fallen sons and fathers. She heard the speeches at the local marketplace, cries of "Heil Hitler" from thin loudspeakers, the crowd spellbound to it all. As a girl, Barbara thought they were saluting "Adolf Fitler". She, her mother and her sister found it painful to watch the return of emaciated prisoners of war after it was all over, many blinded or with missing limbs.

As Barbara grew older and was able to reflect on her experiences she came to realise how much devastation one individual had cast over the whole continent of Europe, with the help of millions of brainwashed citizens. The saving grace for her was that her father, Karl, was never taken in by Nazi propaganda. Instead of capitulating to Hitler, he had delivered a prophetic warning to the people around him. Like Noah, who was ridiculed as he built his ark, Karl built his own house to protect his family from the Allied bombs. Its cellar became a refuge for many of the city's inhabitants. Here in this cellar Barbara played cat's cradle with other children and learned to braid hair. She still owns the card that her father received four years after the war finally came to an end. The yellow document reads "Opfer des Faschismus, Ausweis No. 05535". Attached to it is a photograph of Barbara's father and his ID.

Name: Krätzer
Vorname: Karl
Geboren: 25 12 1903
In: Bad Kreuznach
Kinder: 2 Kinder
Beruf: Schreiner

[The pertinent details are written in three languages: German, French and English.]

The holder of this card belongs to the category of people who in the past years were severely persecuted by the Nazis for political, race, religious reasons. He has been recognised by the committee as a victim of Nazism.
According to article 6b of the Interallied Control.
Landesregierung Rheinland – Pfalz.
Der Minister den Finanzen und für Wiedergutmachung.
Bad Kreuznach, den 18. 02. 1949.
It is recommended to all offices publics and to all authorities to protect the bearer of this legitimation and to facilitate matters as far as it is in any way possible.

The US Army was stationed permanently in Bad Kreuznach until 2001. The American forces erected barracks, a missile store, a shooting range, a small airfield and a military training post. After Barbara left school she worked in a military hospital where she met an American soldier who was half American and half Cherokee. Barbara was attracted to him partly because he symbolised freedom; she longed to embrace the rest of the world and leave Germany behind as soon as possible. She fell in love and became pregnant. Nine months later, in 1957, Barbara gave birth to a daughter, Anette. The soldier visited her and her parents at Ledderhoserweg, held his baby daughter in his arms just once and walked away, disappearing forever. He left a photograph so that when the girl was old enough Barbara could tell her who her father was. He returned to America where he later raised his own family and died in 2008.

In 1960 Barbara met another American soldier in the hospital where she worked on the reception desk. Hugh Cassidy was personable and attractive and he seemed more reliable than Anette's father.

The name Cassidy is old enough to be found in medieval documents. The first Cassidys hailed from the green fields of County Fermanagh in Northern Ireland and in the 19th century many migrated to America where their name still exists as Cassity, Cassedy and Caseda, as well as the original Cassidy. Hugh's forefathers used the original spelling, as did the ancestors of Bill Clinton's mother, also a Cassidy. Local historian PO Gallachair wrote about Hugh's forebears: "Their name was renowned, but unlike most ancient Irish families their fame was never won in mere physical feats of arms, in blood and tears. Theirs was a higher, more noble fame. They were men of peace, culture and scholarship."

Cassidys were prominent in art, medicine and religion. From the 16th century onwards, many medical tracts were authored by ancestors of the Cassidys; a manuscript written by An Giolla Glas Ó Caiside between 1515 and 1527 – a scientific commentary on medicine, philosophy, astronomy and botany – still can be found in the library of Corpus Christi College in Oxford.

The Cassidys also made an impression in poetry and song. 'An Caisideach Ban' is a ballad about a fair-haired Cassidy, its author Tomas Ó Cassidy an 18th-century Augustinian Friar who was expelled from his order on account of a bad marriage. He became a wandering poet and a renegade priest. His famous poem tells the story of Cassidy the priest who lusts after a fair maiden, his final wish on his death bed a kiss from her. It is the sort of melancholy lyric that Eva Cassidy would have loved to sing.

Hugh Cassidy's forefathers migrated to Philadelphia in 1870. Hugh's father, Lewis Cochran Cassidy (1899–1948), won degrees from two prestigious universities in Washington, D.C. and became a law professor. He left his wife, Clara, after the birth of their fourth child and started a new family with a much younger woman. Hugh was just four. Lewis was affluent and sent money to Clara, which provided her children with a good education.

All of them took an avid interest in the arts. Sons John and Lew followed their father into the legal profession, becoming successful attorneys, and benefactors of classical music and theatre in the capital city. Their sister, Isabel, was also talented; she had a fine taste in art and was musical, starting her own choir, and later becoming a school teacher and raising her own children. Talent for the arts seemed to run in the family; Hugh's second cousin, actor Henry Gibson (1935–2009), rose to fame after moving to Hollywood where he was later to take roles in the 1975 Robert Altman film *Nashville* and in TV comedy *Rowan & Martin's Laugh In*.

Hugh's mother, Clara McGrew (1902–1999), was the daughter of James and Eva McGrew. Her father was a wandering priest and her mother accompanied the congregational singing on guitar. After her husband abandoned her Clara dedicated the best part of her life to bringing up her four children as a single mother, working in a department store to earn a living. She could easily have withdrawn in bitterness and frustration but, in fact, she did quite the opposite. In 1960 she bought a small farmhouse in the beautiful small town of Harper's Ferry in the breathtakingly beautiful countryside of West Virginia, a state that was put on the map by John Denver's tribute 'Take Me Home, Country Roads'. A historic town, Harper Ferry's railway junction was destroyed in the Civil War. It is one of several towns through which the famed Appalachian Trail passes.

Clara never remarried and flourished as an extremely independent woman. She was a bright lady and produced an impressive series of publications, becoming a successful author and columnist in later life. She wrote sharp and often witty essays about the joys and burdens of getting older, which were collated into booklets with titles like *Stay Off That Rocker!* One of Clara's best-known books, *We Like Kindergarten*, part of the Little Golden Book series for children, was translated into many languages.

Clara wrote an interesting article in a local paper in 1978 which discussed the Japanese poetic form of haiku and included several revealing self-composed examples. Haiku is a very short form of poetry which traditionally consists of 17 *on* (a sound unit, such as meter in English verse). There are usually three lines, in five, seven and five *on* respectively. In the article, she characterises herself as a lover of nature and gives an account of the repercussions of her experiences of the art: "Just as a wok banishes a cluttered kitchen full of utensils, so the haiku (a small poem of Japanese origin) does away with expensive camera, film, lenses, light meters, tape recorders and bulky souvenirs. Once this simple form of poetry is mastered (and that's quite easy) any moment worth preserving can be captured quickly any time, anywhere with nothing but a pencil and a scrap of paper."

Clara started her personal haiku habit to preserve her memories of her first hike along the Appalachian Trail. For over 20 years she continued to keep a nature diary, preserving not only images made by light and shade, but colour, movement, taste, touch, scent and sound in the form of self-penned haiku. Each memory, with date and place of origin, was recorded in her notebook. Small Comfort, her seven-room farmhouse with four acres of country land in Harper's Ferry, inspired the following haiku:

The sun is setting – Perching
For one bright moment
In my cedar tree

Clara gives several further examples of haiku and concludes: "No expensive equipment. No clutter. No deterioration with the passage of time. No depletion of your store regardless of how much you share it. All of life's sensory delights, the taste of nectar, the scent of mingled wild roses and honeysuckle on a sun-warmed hillside, the gossamer touch of autumn's floating spider silk, the soft plop of a falling ripe plum may be preserved indefinitely by this simple method. Nothing in nature is too minuscule to give the observant onlooker a joy entirely out of proportion to its size... nor to form the subject of a poem. The haiku is entirely consistent with a lifestyle based on the economy of nature... the evanescence may be so delicately crystallised for future enjoyment."

Hugh Cassidy, raised solely by his mother, was sent to boarding schools in Virginia, Tennessee, Florida and Vermont where he encountered a string of bullies, an experience that would affect him for the rest of his life. Hugh and Clara had a difficult relationship – if he didn't obey her she beat him with a leather sandal. Eight years away stymied his ties with home and Hugh's early years were extremely unhappy. He found his joy in solitary trips to the woods, collecting animals and raising rats, guinea pigs, hamsters, lizards and turtles. He started making music on a comb and a piece of paper. Later he took up guitar and mandolin and tried to forget the melancholy days of his youth.

Hugh attended teacher's college in the fifties, and in the latter half of the decade took some time off to pursue music full time, travelling on the road with a band. Drafted into the army in 1959, his military service began in Germany, where he became a male nurse in the military hospital at Bad Kreuznach. It was here that he met Barbara, a young German woman that he liked very much. She recognised in Hugh the same qualities she had seen in her father, and she was attracted to him by the fact that Hugh had intended to make teaching his future profession as in Germany at that time teachers were held in very high regard. In March 1961, just three months after they met, they were married. Hugh accepted Barbara's firstborn, Anette, as if she were his own and the family took to life under the clay roof of the house on the hill in the outskirts of Bad Kreuznach. Their daughter Margret was born there in 1962.

Barbara still dreamed of flying away to America. A year after Margret's birth Hugh's German duty was over and he took his family back to the United States and an uncertain future. They travelled in a propeller aircraft; a long journey in a relatively slow plane and throughout the trip Margret sat on her mother's lap. Along with Anette and Margret, Barbara was also carrying her third, as yet unborn, child over the ocean.

Eva Marie Cassidy was born on February 2, 1963 at 10.00 p.m. in the Washington Hospital Center in Washington, D.C. Her first name was taken from Hugh's grandmother, Eva McGrew, the Christian singer and guitar player.

The family's first year in the city was spent in the Southeast area in Washington, D.C., where they lived on the third floor of a small brick apartment on 1st Street. At that time the area had a predominantly white population and many who saw little Eva were enchanted by her blonde hair and her bright blue eyes. Neighbours gave her the nickname Miss Sunshine. A year later they moved to Martin Luther King Boulevard. During their first few years in America the family had to get by on what little money Barbara had saved in Germany. Hugh tried to make a living as a musician and he also studied to become a teacher.

An early family portrait from the sixties reveals much about the young Cassidy family. In the black and white photograph Eva is positioned on her father's thigh. Hugh looks into the camera with the confidence of a former serviceman, his head adorned with an elegant and flamboyant quiff. The sleeves of his checkered shirt cover only half of his muscled arms. Hugh's impressive shoulders portray confidence, his left arm tenderly cradling the shoulders of his daughter. Eva seems uneasy, though. She looks a bit frightened and, to a degree, somewhere outside the reach of the camera.

Next to Hugh on the couch are mother Barbara and Eva's older sister, Margret. Barbara looks admiringly at her husband, her eyes partly hidden behind the dark spectacle frames popular in that decade. The position of the venetian blinds is significant: they are pulled down, but left slightly open – welcoming, but only to visitors who are kindly. The members of the family are oriented towards each other. The design of the room seems modest. Behind Hugh's impressively broad back is a small row of books on the windowsill. That Hugh radiates so much power and quietness is not unexpected; he was a family man, but he skipped dinner twice a week to practise power lifting. Family photographs in colour from a later period show Hugh's impressively muscular torso amid the breakers at Ocean City, Maryland, or with his strong arms wrapped around Eva. She wears a red bathing suit and stares into the camera with a mixture of trust and trepidation, perhaps betraying the fact that she was somewhat intimidated by her father's presence even at that early age.

For one terrible moment Eva's life came dangerously close to ending when she fell down in her crib, landing with her head caught between the railings. Barbara heard Eva cry out and ran into the bedroom where she was confronted by the sight of her little daughter hanging by her neck, her face turning blue. Barbara pulled her from the railings and, putting her medical background into action, administered mouth-to-mouth resuscitation, effectively saving her life. Eva was rushed to hospital, suffering convulsions en route. After several days' stay tests showed there was no serious damage, and she was discharged. Barbara's courageous act marked the beginning of an unusually close bond between mother and daughter.

Chapter 2

Blue Skies

Eva's brother, Dan, was born in 1964, the same year that the family moved to a detached house with a small piece of land in Oxon Hill, a few miles east of the D.C. border in the state of Maryland. The best thing that could be said of this dormant suburb was that it was quiet and that there was plenty of space for the children to play.

Hugh finished his teacher training and found work as a special education teacher in an elementary school. Barbara took care of the children and the housekeeping. The children were by no means brought up strictly, but their parents considered it important for the family to dine together, the only exception to this rule being the evenings when Hugh's power lifting or musical activities took him out of the house. He had serious aspirations to become a champion power lifter and as a semi-professional musician he commanded regular gigs around town.

Hugh and Barbara shared a passion for nature, and tried to pass this love on to their children, who played outside constantly and enjoyed the family's Sunday walks. Soon the children could recite the names of most of the plants and trees in their neighbourhood. Their favorite destination was Cedarville, a beautiful park with cedar trees and a lovely promenade walk around a pond. Eva put together bouquets of flowers that she picked during these walks and she grew her own fruit and vegetables in a small patch in the garden.

Anette evolved into the outsider of the family as time went on: she was older than the other children and didn't share a biological father. Initially, Eva and Margret were very close but as Dan grew older the bond between him and Eva strengthened. Their emotional ties became clear when Eva stayed away from home for a few days and Dan cried: "I want my Eva back!"

Eva's favourite toy was Suzie Cute, a small plastic doll with nylon hair that she placed in a rocking cradle made from wood. Suzie slept under a red and white gingham blanket, her eyes half closed and her arms stretched in Eva's direction most of the time.

Barbara encouraged her daughter's creative skills by giving her pencils, paper and coloured chalk. At two years old Eva produced drawings that, although childlike, demonstrated she had talent. The little figures she drew were simple, but they showed real movement and a degree of emotion. When Eva worked she concentrated hard, not allowing herself to be interrupted. She was as playful and boisterous as any other child, but she found comfort by withdrawing into her own creative world.

A very important book for Eva was *The Story Of The Root-Children* by Sibylle von Olfers and she pleaded with Barbara to read it to her every night at bedtime. She loved the story and absorbed the illustrations, her early drawing style inspired by the fairy-like pictures of children and insects she found in its pages. It ignited a lifelong conviction: killing an insect was to be as frowned upon as killing any other living creature.

The children needed only to cross the street to get to school. The teachers at Oxon Hill's primary school, Owens Road Elementary, were pleasantly surprised by Eva's artistic talent and often showed her drawings to the other children as an example of what could be achieved. Eva's siblings admired the fact that Eva was able to draw so fluently and make her characters so lifelike.

Barbara's determination to give her children an education in art and culture was partly inspired by her own childhood in Bad Kreuznach, which was far from sophisticated. She was constantly amazed by the opportunities to view so many impressive works of art in the galleries and museums of Washington, D.C., just a few miles from the family home.

The National Gallery of Art, located on The Mall, boasts three separate areas: the stately, classical West Building, the modern triangular East Building and The Sculpture Garden. The East Building holds a huge collection of modern art and The Sculpture Garden not only displays the very best of American sculpture but offers visitors many examples of plants and trees native to America. There was no entrance fee, which made it an excellent way to broaden the children's visual horizons.

At that time only the neoclassical West Building had been built. The impressive entrance to the large marble building, which is centred around a domed rotunda modelled on the Pantheon in Rome, must have overwhelmed the children. The gallery houses a vast collection of paintings, drawings, prints, photographs, sculptures, medals and decorative arts.

In the gallery, Eva was exposed to the old masters. She loved Giotto's *Madonna And Child*, an important example of the transition from classical painting to the Renaissance, which shows a mother's affection for her offspring. Leonardo da Vinci's work inspired her and she tried to copy the *Mona Lisa*, the world-famous painting that never leaves the Musée du Louvre in Paris. However, Eva had the chance to admire firsthand another of his mysterious models: *Ginevra de' Benci,* completed in 1474 and the only Leonardo in the Americas. Eva was also attracted by the romanticism of Claude Monet who painted *Woman With Umbrella*, a depiction of his wife holding a parasol and their son, in 1875. James McNeill Whistler painted his mistress, Joanna Hiffernan, in a stunning white dress in 1862 for *Symphony In White, No. 1: The White Girl.* Eva was especially fascinated by the Dutch masters. It's not difficult to see why: Rembrandt van Rhijn is well known for his oil paintings, but experts allude to his etchings as "the real thing", the extraordinary compassion and affection that Rembrandt brought to his work. In his 1637 etching *Abraham Casting Out Hagar And Ishmael,* you can sense the heart-wrenching moment when Sarah ordered her husband, Abraham, to send his mistress, Hagar, and her son, Ishmael, into the desert. It's a refined picture, but even at a young age Eva had developed a sharp eye for injustice and she must have shivered at the thought of what Hagar and her son had gone through.

The National Gallery also owns paintings by Johannes Vermeer, of which the best is almost certainly *Girl With A Red Hat*, circa 1665–1666. Dutch artists are known for their use of contrasting light and this painting is a perfect example of the use of colour, its three bold strips of red, white and blue reminiscent of the Dutch flag.

The gallery displays several paintings by Vincent van Gogh (1853–1890), the Dutch painter who lived completely for his art. Vivid colours and emotional impact are characteristic of a painter who suffered from anxiety and frequent bouts of mental illness throughout his life, dying largely unknown at the age of 37 from a self-inflicted gunshot wound. Van Gogh's fame grew steadily among colleagues, art critics, dealers and collectors and by the mid-20th century he was credited as one of the greatest painters in history, his best work powerful enough to convince any observer of its timeless quality. Van Gogh's *Self Portrait 1889* shows the contrast between the dark blue of his smock and the red of his hair and beard. The dynamic brushwork gives an intense expression to his tormented face. Eva liked Van Gogh's innocent *Roulin's Baby* of 1888, a lovely painting with a green background. Eva loved green in paintings, the colour of nature and the countryside.

Barbara didn't talk much in the museum: she wanted her children to experience these works of art without disturbance, but on the way home she recounted Van Gogh's tragic life to an entranced Eva.

At the end of each visit the children were allowed to choose a postcard displaying their favorite work of art. Dan showed a morbid preference for the surreal works of Spanish master Salvador Dali, especially those of his skeletons. Eva asked for postcards of the Dutch masters and Barbara, a serious promoter of art, bought them for her without hesitating.

Eva's creative skills went hand in hand with her high sensitivity. She could talk for days about a pitiful person she had seen on television and she developed a somewhat exaggerated propensity towards the need for justice. When she and her brother or sisters misbehaved, like all children sometimes do, Eva always took the blame when they were caught. She wasn't a gossip, she didn't tell tales and she would wrap everything in the cloak of charity. But anger needs an outlet every now and then and Eva sometimes suffered from sudden fits when her suppressed anger burst out. Barbara called these tantrums her "Rumpelstiltskin acts", a reference to the impish character in the German fairy tale of the same name, written by the Brothers Grimm and first published in 1812. However, Eva's anger was always expressed at objects, never at other people.

Whereas Barbara nurtured the development of Eva's artistic skills, Hugh can take credit for the musical influences in Eva's life. Hugh and Barbara were both music lovers and their modern stereo record player was in use for most of the day. Their huge record collection included acoustic folk music of the Folkways Collections, Leadbelly, The Weavers, Judy Collins, Pete and Peggy Seeger and Bob Dylan's 1967 *Greatest Hits* album, which was a favourite. Eva and her siblings knew the chorus to 'Rainy Day Women #12 & 35' – "Everybody must get stoned" – by heart and would sing along with real verve, despite not knowing the real meaning of the lyrics. Eva adored the Cree Indian singer Buffy Sainte-Marie, especially her song 'I'm Gonna Be A Country Girl Again'. The moment she saw a photograph of Sainte-Marie in front of a microphone and wearing headphones she realised she wanted to be a singer.

Anette used to bring home singles and LP records of up to date pop music she liked and the Cassidys always showed an interest in her records. Hugh had started out on upright bass in the late fifties, playing whatever music he could to earn money, but in 1959 he switched to the electric bass guitar, investing in a Fender Precision, the most popular instrument of its kind, to play in rock'n'roll groups. He was also proficient on acoustic guitar and mandolin. At Christmas 1971, Hugh bought a Seals & Crofts album called *Year Of Sunday*, which the family all loved. It was the most contemporary record they had ever heard, and they were especially enamoured with the song 'Year Of Sunday', which had religious overtones that appealed to Eva, Dan and Margret.

When relatives visited the Cassidy home the children and Hugh would give a musical performance. Their speciality was three- or four-part harmonies and they had great success with the barbershop-styled 'Tell Me Why The Stars Do Shine'. Harmonising was second nature to the children, especially Eva who took a leading role when they practised melodies. As soon as she heard a tune on the car radio or on the television she would sing a second part. During their practice, Hugh trained Eva's musical ear further by calling "And now in a different key!"

In 1972, the family moved to a larger house in Bowie, Maryland, a rural town some 15 miles from Oxon Hill. The extra space meant they could keep animals, including ducks, pigs, turtles and even an opossum, and their father built a beehive and a hobby shed in the garden. The children attended High Bridge Elementary School, while Barbara began working several hours a week, first at a Christmas shop and later at Behnke's Garden Nursery in Beltsville.

Eva, then aged nine, was shaken by the move. She dealt with this radical change by drawing endlessly and developing an interest in ceramics. Her teachers were surprised at her seemingly effortless and prolific creativity and she was asked to paint a mural on the wall of a classroom, which is still there today.

Her musical education continued to flourish, and one particularly significant moment came during a school concert. Adrienne Savage, a black girl from a poor family whose house had burned down on Thanksgiving, sang 'Put Your Hand In The Hand', a gospel song with secular elements. Adrienne had, in fact, behaved arrogantly towards the Cassidy children in the past, but her voice and style of singing made a huge impression on Eva.

Aunt Isabel gave Eva her first instrument: an autoharp. It was easy to play and produced immediate results, since complete chords could be played with just one finger. Eva began to accompany herself on dozens of songs, a great step forward. She quickly mastered the instrument, although the limited range of chords restricted her progress. However, a year later Hugh gave her a real musical instrument: an easy to play Harmony guitar with nylon strings, on which he taught her the basics.

The first song that Eva taught herself to play and sing was 'I Wish I Was A Single Girl Again', a song that would become a fixture in her repertoire at later concerts. As she learned more about the guitar she discovered the charms of sharp, flat, diminished and half-diminished chords. In the same year that they moved to Bowie, Dan got his first violin. He chose the instrument because he'd seen a boy in his class play the theme from the McDonald's commercial from memory, which certainly impressed the young boy.

Eva and Dan often played together. Dan developed more control over his bow, enabling him to produce an authentic and melancholy sound that was perfect for the folk music they preferred. Buffy Sainte-Marie's 'Tall Trees In Georgia' became a firm favourite, and another song that Eva sang and played around this time was 'Long Long Time', by country songwriter Gary White, which had been covered by Linda Ronstadt on her 1970 album *Silk Purse* and, released as a single, reached number 25 in the *Billboard* charts, her first hit. "This was quite an accomplished feat at her age to learn to sing this and accompany herself," says Dan. "She and I played this many times together. She also liked a ballad by Bonnie Raitt called 'Love Has No Pride' and learned it around a year later. These were two quite important songs in her development as a singer/guitarist because they have more than a few chords and she experimented with phrasing quite a bit with her singing and developed that skill with these songs."

'Love Has No Pride' was also covered by Ronstadt, and was a highlight of her 1973 album *Don't Cry Now*.

Aside from indulging their love of music and high culture in the Washington museums and art galleries, the children spent a good deal of time in front of the family television. Eva was glued to the coverage of the 1972 Olympic Games in Munich and she adored watching gymnast Cathy Rigby, to the point where she took up gymnastics herself for several months.

One of Eva's earliest favourites was *The Sonny & Cher Show*. Eva and Margret idolised Cher and were angry at their mother for not allowing them to wear their hair like the famous singer. Nevertheless, they imitated Cher in front of their mirror. Lacking Cher's long hair, they draped towels over their heads and secretly used Hugh's shoe polish in an attempt to achieve its jet black colour.

Eva found television and film important windows to the world and she loved the classic Hollywood stars Fred Astaire, Ginger Rogers and Mickey Rooney, and nostalgic films such as *The Bowery Boys* and programmes like *The Little Rascals*.

Her favourite film, however, was *The Wizard Of Oz*, which was broadcast at least once a year. Each time it was announced in *TV Guide* the children worked themselves into a state of excitement that lasted for several days. The film, made in 1937, had an incomparable effect on all of the children, but especially Eva, who was transported by the fantasy and atmosphere of the story. She was 10 years old when she first heard Judy Garland sing 'Over The Rainbow', and it touched her deeply.

More than 70 years after filming Judy Garland's performance is still magical. As Dorothy, Garland walks into a farmyard that evokes the Garden of Eden; a chicken runs freely and there is no sign of anyone else as she begins to sing. Her black plaits hang around her face, giving her an innocent, girlish appearance. Dorothy's dog, Toto, scurries towards her and the scene culminates in the dog presenting its paw to the ecstatically singing girl. It's a touching sight: nothing can beat an animal's loyalty. It represents a life without fear or pain, which is reflected in those famous lyrics that express a universal desire to leave all misery behind and arrive at an imaginary fairyland, where skies are always blue and where dreams, however unrealistic, come true. Problems melt away in this beautiful land at the end of the rainbow, and in its expression of craving for a better world, it took on almost religious proportions within Eva Cassidy.

In November 1971, Hugh, weighing in at 300lbs, took the title of World Champion Super Heavyweight power lifter. It was the last medal he would win; the sport led to him injuring his leg but he would continue to be involved as a coach. In the same year, the family home was redecorated by a house painter called Leo who spent several weeks with the Cassidy family. He was an unconventional character, quite unlike anyone who had crossed their paths before, with an alternative slant on the world, a casual dress sense and a beard, which was fairly radical in Oxon Hill at that time. The Cassidy children took to him immediately and Eva, who always kept a certain distance when she met new people, was charmed by the remarkable painter. Leo had a disarming nature: he was not a chatterbox, which would have put Eva off. The children gave him the pet name "Leo with the Beard". In the early seventies Eva had begun to paint with water colours and she observed closely the way Leo used his brush.

Although a house painter by profession, Leo painted canvasses in his spare time. Hugh encouraged Eva to visit Leo at his home so that he could teach her how to paint. Afraid to go alone, Eva asked her brother, Dan, to join her. Both were welcomed into Leo's eccentric home, which was decorated with a mix of Leo's own paintings and several native objects from Africa where he and his partner, an attractive hippie girl, had lived for some years. The smell of turpentine in the house competed with the aroma of incense. Dan and Eva felt immediately at ease with the unorthodox couple. Having never travelled beyond the state of Maryland, they listened to their stories about far away continents with growing fascination.

Leo showed the young siblings how to paint with oils. It was the first time that they had ever seen a real artist at work. Dan noticed that Leo was the first grown-up with whom Eva felt completely at ease.

There was another side to Leo that was new to Dan and Eva: he was a Christian missionary who felt his purpose was to visit the continent of Africa to convert Africans to Christianity. Dan and Eva didn't know much about Christianity, since Hugh and Barbara were Democrats who disliked the so-called Republican Evangelicals. It was a great surprise to Dan and Eva that a low profile, shabbily dressed fellow like Leo called himself a Christian. He was serious about it, too: this cheerful and talkative character was also a preacher.

Leo seemed almost too good to be true, and Eva and Dan's curiosity was piqued. When he was certain that they were prepared for commitment, he asked them to join him and his wife at the church where he was minister but before they could attend, the children required the approval of their non church-going parents. Barbara and Hugh were also surprised by Leo's dedication to the ministry, but since they liked the house painter, they gave their blessing for their children to go along. Margret was similarly curious, so Leo and his wife picked up all three Cassidy siblings in their car the following Sunday morning, Barbara having given them some change for the offertory.

What Leo had referred to as a church actually turned out to be a very simple apartment on the edge of Washington, D.C. The building was old and tired, the carpet worn down to almost nothing. Most of the congregation was black; in fact Leo, his wife, Dan, Margret and Eva were the only white people present. The Cassidy children didn't know where to look at first, then listened in astonishment to Leo's sermon.

Leo was a gifted speaker who appealed to the emotions of his audience in the way that Baptist preachers are wont to do. Eva was especially receptive to Leo's message – Dan and Margret noticed with amazement that tears ran down her cheeks. Later the nine-year-old Eva would explain that they had been tears of joy because she had suddenly realised that people should always treat others in the same way the churchgoers respected each other. It touched her and comforted her at the same time. But there was something else that contributed to Eva's tears: her compassion towards oppressed minorities. Leo preached "God has liberated the black people from slavery and from injustice" and Eva listened intently, shocked by the cruelty inflicted in the past by white people on their black brothers and sisters.

The atmosphere in Leo's church was one of love and care for others. Some of the congregation didn't speak a word of English, yet they understood Leo's message and smiled constantly, despite their often desperate circumstances. (Barbara had actually given the children light bulbs to offer because the "poor people all the way from Africa" might need them someday.) The children were inspired and felt welcome in this building – there was warmth and happiness here which reflected the Cassidy mindset. They knew little of this new world with its secret codes, messages and odd manner of speech, but the most important thing was that the other churchgoers didn't judge them.

The Cassidy siblings continued to attend Sunday services so their usual walks with their parents were postponed to later in the day. Hugh and Barbara were somewhat surprised by their children's newfound enthusiasm for worship, but they reasoned that it wouldn't harm them.

Another aspect of the church services that appealed to the Cassidys was the music. In the shady apartment in the Washingtonian outskirts there was much enthusiastic singing of hymns and other songs of praise. It was here that Eva first came upon the true quality of black music: black voices simply sounded better than their white counterparts. From thereon in, Eva, Dan and Margret absorbed black music on TV and radio and they were particularly taken with the positive and uplifting music of gospel. The sound, full of emotion and feeling, enveloped Eva and she was able to escape into her own little world, something she would continue to do throughout her life.

Pastor "Leo with the Beard" became a professional promoter of the Christian message and was soon asked to work for a larger congregation in a real church in the east of D.C. Margret, Eva and Dan followed him. There, the choir and the church band were even better, and the building was immaculate, with many seats, a good sound system and a real baptism font. Leo worked alongside Pastor McMillan who was most interested in these unusual worshippers, the first children he had ever seen visit his church without their parents. He encouraged them to attend Sunday school lessons to learn more about the stories of the Bible.

The Sunday school was run by several sisters, and Dan, Margret and Eva enjoyed the attention they received from them as they carefully built the children's faith. Eva and Margret were asked to look as delighted as if they were in heaven. Using the power of their vivid imaginations, they were suddenly overwhelmed by happiness. "Would you like to experience this deep joy forever?" the sisters asked them. They didn't have to think twice; deep in their hearts they knew that a life without problems was unimaginable, but the sisters acted as if eternal happiness really was possible.

The sisters explained the connection between the stories in the Bible and life. "We are victims of our poor situation but we can be saved," the ladies explained. "If you are willing to accept the fact that you can't help yourself but that you need heavenly support, you should join us and be baptised." Eva and Margret looked at each other. They were ready to take the plunge.

Eva and Margret were treated as adopted children of the church. They didn't belong to a Christian family, but they would now become members of the spiritual family of the Capitol Baptist Church. Like the founding Protestant church father Martin Luther said: "The power, effect, benefit, fruit and purpose of Baptism is to save. No one is baptised in order to become a prince, but as the words say, to be 'saved'. This is nothing else than to be delivered from sin, death, and the devil and to enter the kingdom of Christ and live with him forever."

Hugh and Barbara's absence during the ceremony was unusual. Dan (who was too young to be baptised) was the only member of the Cassidy family who witnessed the baptism ceremony of Margret and Eva. After they had answered "yes" to the questions during the liturgy they came forward to the little pool at the front of the church. The preacher submersed them completely under water for a few seconds. Eva was not usually one for the spotlight, but in this moment she discovered a profound sense of well-being.

Chapter 3

Don't Show Your Ignorance

It is April 2, 1978, and while owner Jack lights the hearth fire and bartender Brian rinses the glasses, three musicians enter the Fleet Reserve Club through the back entrance. The attractive club in the historic town of Annapolis in Chesapeake Bay, Maryland, is usually the preserve of navy personnel during the evening hours. "Whatever happens Dan, don't show your ignorance," Eva carefully reminds her brother. Usually he chuckles at their favourite quote from TV series *The Rascals*, but tonight they are both too tense to laugh. Hugh walks like a man in charge, acting as though the Fleet Reserve is his natural habitat. He had decided the time is right to present his musical children to an audience of strangers.

Hugh has had trouble finding a parking lot near to the club, so the trio are a bit late. The first guests can arrive any moment. When Hugh takes off his coat the enormous bundle of muscles under his Hawaiian shirt attract attention. Eva asks Dan if he can stand between her and her father on the flat stage. Hugh positions the house microphones, shifts the monitor loudspeakers a bit and moves a bar stool so that he can sit while playing. Dan tunes his violin at the same time. Eva looks a bit lost in this unfamiliar space and she stares at the ground. "Put on your

Behind The Rainbow: The Tragic Life Of Eva Cassidy

dress," commands Hugh, who notices his daughter daydreaming. "Ask Jack where you can find the dressing room."

They have practised at home for years; they know the "American songbook" practically by heart. They begin a warm-up. Eva, who has the best voice, takes lead vocals. Dan and Hugh pluck a second and a third part out of the air. With the same ease Dan conjures up attractive counter-melodies from his violin. Hugh is convinced that his teenage children will create a stir among the audience. Later that evening accordion player Joe and his pregnant wife will join them in a few songs. Dan and especially Eva would have preferred to stay at home but Hugh is unrelenting: "Don't bury your talents in the ground and don't hide your light under a bushel."

While they wait to start the show, Dan and Eva quietly sit at the bar, each with a glass of Pepsi. They study the pictures of famous predecessors hanging from the walls, not least the celebrated Virginian jazz guitarist Charlie Byrd and his brother Joe. When Jack gives Hugh a signal he urges his children to get up and take their positions on the small stage. Eva is the last to leave the bar, as Hugh planned, yet her face betrays her nerves. Someone shouts through the loudspeakers: "A big hand for the Cassidy family," but Eva isn't able to see where the voice comes from. She tries to loosen her guitar, tuned by Hugh, from its stand, but she realises that the strap is stuck. Eva's black dress takes away much of her freedom of movement, yet she knows there is no alternative but to squat down and try to release the strap. "Use your vibrato," Hugh whispers piercingly from behind his electric bass guitar. But Eva is more concerned with the ungraceful position she has assumed. With all the power in her short arms, she succeeds in dislodging the strap so that she is finally able to hang the Harmony guitar with the nylon strings round her neck. She can't postpone the confrontation with her audience any longer. When she turns around she stands transfixed as the microphone and stand drop to the wooden floor with a loud bang, causing a painful and penetrating screech of reverb.

It was while the Cassidy family was living in Bowie that the children met a lady by the name of Mrs Near, who lived in Largo, Maryland,

24

and happened to be a regular churchgoer. She and her two grown-up unmarried daughters asked Eva, Dan and Margret to join them at their church. The Cassidy children welcomed any opportunity to escape the difficulties of everyday life, and accepted the invitation, hoping to enter the same bubble as that of the black churches in Washington, D.C.

Every Sunday morning the Nears pulled up outside the Cassidys' house and honked the horn. The children piled in, their destination the Capitol Baptist Church in Largo, a solid but rather austere building in complete contrast to Leo's warm church in D.C. Here, the congregation was white, well off and smartly dressed in expensive clothes and polished shoes. The music was also different: no hand clapping, no black gospel, no choir, just the Calvinist asceticism of a very white-sounding electronic organ accompanying slow, old-fashioned hymns. Unlike Leo, Pastor Cooper didn't preach about the liberation of slavery and injustice but held forth on the low and sinful state of mankind.

In the beginning they were welcomed into the new church, the red carpet rolled out for them, and they eagerly awaited the horn-honking on Sunday mornings. But as they became integrated into the church the worshippers began to expect certain niceties from them and, in a manner of speaking, they were subjected to the same kind of harsh treatment they had received at the hands of their fellow school pupils. Their shoes weren't sufficiently polished, the girls preferred trousers and large sweaters to dresses, Dan's hair was too long for a boy. "Leo with the Beard" and Pastor McMillan had taught them about the beauty of the Christian faith, but Pastor Cooper preached fire and brimstone. They were flabbergasted that the two communities could differ so much from each other, and it had a huge effect on them. Dan found it difficult to sleep because he was afraid he would end up in eternal hellfire.

On top of this the rides to Largo were becoming uncomfortable. The children were growing in height and it was far from easy to get six people into the Nears' small car. It was cramped, muggy and oppressive and they had difficulty breathing. It all got too much, and one day they decided not to go to church any more. They didn't like to tell Mrs Near personally, so they asked Barbara to make the difficult phone call.

★

Many children experience the transition from primary school to secondary education as a fundamental change in their lives, the move from childhood to something approaching adulthood. For Eva Cassidy the passage to junior high was nothing less than a disaster. Their neighbourhood in Bowie was quiet, white and prosperous. At the time when Eva left primary school, the government was in the throes of an attempt to reduce segregation between the different sections of the town's population. Children in Bowie were forced to attend Robert Goddard Junior High School in Lanham, a poor area three miles east of New Carrollton, not far from the Goddard Space Centre. The Cassidy children were taken six miles by school bus every weekday. Suddenly they belonged to a middle-class minority in a school of hundreds.

Eva had always found change difficult to deal with, but a crowded school in a rough part of town was almost too much to bear. So she became an outsider, a creative recluse. At primary school other children had thought it charming that Eva lost herself in art and music, but the pupils at junior high lacked this tolerance and cultural consciousness. Some of those at Robert Goddard were raw, harsh and ill-mannered; the lives of many of Eva's 12-year-old classmates consisted largely of hanging around on the streets, smoking and making out in rough parts of town. Eva was annoyed by their lack of manners and disinterest in the curriculum. Many of her classmates were shockingly superficial, interested only in clothes and sport. Hugh and Barbara watched their daughter transform from a bright and breezy child into a dejected teenager, retreating within herself in her small bedroom.

The other children at the school noticed how Eva was changing and they didn't understand her. The problem wasn't that she was ignored, but they couldn't stand the fact that Eva refused to adapt. Driven by group mentality, they feared anyone who stood out from the crowd and though the peer pressure to conform was enormous, Eva simply didn't want to be a part of it. Her classmates started to bully her. Eva's first year in junior high was a defining period of her life, a clear turning point. The world was not as wonderful as she had thought or hoped. Eva was unequivocally ousted from her childhood paradise.

Despite the indifference of her classmates, Eva continued to draw and paint. She was particularly honoured when asked to design the cover of the annual school yearbook. However, indifference turned to blind hatred when they discovered how important art was to Eva and her work became the object of petty vandalism. On one occasion Eva had worked for hours on a painting that showed the first traces of real talent, winning much praise from her teacher. The same day, jealous fellow pupils ruined the painting by throwing drops of paint on the canvas, claiming it was an accident.

Eva began to cry in public when she didn't know how to defend herself against this kind of ill-treatment. The word "fight" wasn't a part of her vocabulary because she simply didn't want to struggle; she didn't need to win. She merely wanted to be left alone to be herself. It's no surprise that Eva's uncertainty about herself and others gained ground during this period. She began to lose the motivation to do her best at school, although she continued to complete her homework through a sense of duty. Instead, she would draw in lessons, sometimes producing cartoons of the teachers, but also crafting the recognisable reproduction of Leonardo da Vinci's *Mona Lisa*.

In 1973, the Murphys, an Anglo-Indian family, emigrated from India to Maryland. Their children, Ruth and Celia, were enrolled at Robert Goddard Junior High School where they attended music classes supervised by Rosemary Rockwell. Eva and Margret attended Rosemary's choir lessons and met up with Ruth and Celia. The Murphy sisters loved to sing and they recognised a kindred spirit in Eva.

Eva was welcomed into the class because she could play guitar. She had a great voice but she didn't like to sing solo parts; she was too shy. Scott from Winston-Salem, in North Carolina, had the pleasure of knowing Eva in high school and singing with her in the small choral group. Later he would post an appraisal of Eva on an internet forum: "Often one doesn't recognize great talent amongst seven other singers but everyone recognized Eva's capacity for humility and compassion. As a very quiet person she tried to blend in. She did not seek centre stage and shied away from requests to do solos. Even though she was an excellent choral member, every so often the power and beauty of her voice would overshadow everyone else in the room.

"One particular moment stands out in my mind when our director was frustrated in trying to get a certain passion and depth of sound from us and, being typical teenagers, we were unwilling to put forth the effort. During the next pass through, however, one voice rose above all others, strong, passionate, and with a pristine clarity I'd never heard before in that room. To everyone's surprise, perhaps even to herself, it was Eva. She immediately turned red, looked to the floor, and timidly offered 'I guess I took in a large breath and it wanted out'. Our performance of that song gained new fever and became one of our best. She had shown us just how good it could be. I guess few of us really understood the depth of her talent and her ability to communicate through her singular voice. Even as a teenage person, she was as beautiful and sensitive as her voice. Personally I am blessed to have known her, together we are all fortunate to have these remembrances of her talent and sensitivity."

The choir sang all kinds of music, including hymns, spirituals and folk songs such as 'The Water Is Wide'. Eva wasn't too keen on Mrs Rockwell's no-nonsense approach to music because she couldn't stand strict people, but Margret was different: she liked the straightforward choir leader.

Eva and Celia also joined a folk group that rehearsed after school, led by Ms Bush, a talkative lady and a devout Christian who played guitar and knew many folk songs. It was here that Eva learned what was to become a favourite song, 'Wade In The Water'. One day she brought Mrs Rockwell's songbook home. It covered all kinds of pop songs, including 'Eleanor Rigby'. From then on The Beatles became Dan's favourite band, but although Eva liked some of their songs, she was never a great fan of The Beatles.

Ruth and Celia became Eva's first friends in junior high, a friendship that would last into adulthood. Celia was a year older than both Ruth and Eva, so the bond between the younger girls was tighter. Ruth had an extrovert personality and connected easily with others. Her spontaneity inspired confidence in Eva.

From an early age Ruth always had a circle of friends around her. Eva didn't know how to react in a group, clamming up completely in large gatherings of people. She often asked Ruth if they could do something "together", meaning without others. Ruth respected this, despite the fact that Eva's possessiveness put off her other friends. She had a delicately developed understanding of other people's thoughts and feelings and she quickly saw Eva as a loner who suffered from fits of depression, even at her young age.

Ruth's older sister Celia discovered Eva's clingy nature the hard way. On one occasion Eva asked her to go shopping, but later that day Celia received a phone call from another friend with the same invitation. Without thinking she asked the second friend to join them. When Eva discovered this she reacted angrily and didn't utter a word to Celia for days.

Later, the bond between Celia and Eva would grow, but in junior high Eva preferred Ruth's company, stating, "Celia just doesn't understand all the fun." Ruth and Eva went to the cinema together on a regular basis and also visited museums and galleries. They explored the neighbourhood on their bikes. Eva appreciated Ruth's social skills and regularly poured out her heart to her motherly friend. The fact that Eva could trust a person implicitly in a one-to-one situation marked this relationship out as something special. Ruth got to see Eva free of her fears and inhibitions. It's easy to spot Eva in her yearbook photos, because she is the only one who isn't smiling. With her peers surrounding her she found it impossible to show spontaneity, but when Ruth was alone with Eva she discovered a different, often hidden, side to her personality: this side of Eva could be funny and was able to laugh loudly, and sometimes she even did crazy things.

The girls also had serious talks, sometimes discussing racial discrimination and the inequality of the sexes. As the girls reached the age when boys began to take notice of them, Eva resented being judged, while Ruth saw flirting as a game that could flavour, enlighten and enhance her life. To Eva, life was not a joke and love was serious, like her art and music. Eva was disgusted when girls behaved provocatively, or if they wore clothes designed to attract male attention to their emerging bodies. These matters were more than mere trifles for Eva. They touched her personally and depressed her.

Eva also confided in Ruth about her relationship with her father. Hugh had expressed disappointment with Eva's lack of ambition, her laxity in domestic matters and her lean school results. It wasn't easy for Eva to deal with her father's criticism but his opinion was also important to her. She needed his approval and felt duty bound to accept the sharp edge of his tongue. Eva's attitude towards her father was paradoxical: she hated his scolding, but would turn out to be an even greater perfectionist than he had ever been.

Ruth's importance to Eva is reflected in what she wrote in Ruth's yearbook: "You were the only one, the only friend who understood me, you were the only friend I had this year." She underlined this message with an impressive original drawing of an Indian queen.

As time went on, Hugh Cassidy introduced his children to several albums that gradually shifted their interest from acoustic folk to more solid electric rock. Favourites included Bonnie Raitt, Emmylou Harris and albums such as Linda Ronstadt's hits collection *A Retrospective*, Fleetwood Mac's *Rumours* and The Eagles' *Desperado*.

Linda Ronstadt and Eva had one thing in common: they didn't write songs but interpreted them. However, Linda Ronstadt emphasised her femininity in a way that betrayed her southern background. In the seventies, the walls of many a boy's bedroom were adorned with a poster of Ronstadt dressed in skimpy shorts or a breathtaking off-the-shoulder white blouse. Eva would later cover the Buddy Holly song 'It Doesn't Matter Anymore' in the same style as Ronstadt, but she would never adopt her style of dress.

Linda Ronstadt was accompanied by the band that would later become The Eagles, whose 1973 album *Desperado* is soft country rock, with layered harmonies and exceptional guitar solos. Fleetwood Mac, on the other hand, originated in England but after one of many hiatuses changed their line-up in California with the addition of Lindsey Buckingham and Stevie Nicks. Dan and Eva loved music from the American West Coast, playing Fleetwood Mac's 'Rhiannon' and 'Don't Stop' endlessly.

Another of their songs, 'Songbird', written by their pianist Christine McVie, would later become inextricably linked to Eva.

Eva's room was the smallest bedroom in the house, yet she began to spend more and more time alone there. Nobody knew exactly what she did in her room, but she produced many drawings and she played her guitar for hours on end, perfecting her technique. Completely lost in her own creative universe, she felt comfortable, content to keep the ugly and often hostile external world that asked so much of her at a distance.

Hugh and Barbara regretted that their daughter secluded herself so often, but in hindsight these lonely years were fruitful. Eva listened to a lot of music that was new and unknown to her: the soul of Aretha Franklin, Buffy Sainte-Marie's folk songs and the jazz of Sarah Vaughan and Ella Fitzgerald. She imitated these singers; Joan Baez, for example, taught her how to use vibrato, something that Hugh was constantly hammering her to develop. Fitzgerald, a huge influence for more than a year, would later help Eva to learn improvisation and scatting.

Eva's biggest influence remains unknown to this day. As youngsters, the siblings heard a female singer's voice on a commercial and they fell in love with it; the voice was timeless, ageless and colourless. Eva tried to capture this unique sound and, indeed, these qualities are what Eva has become known for. Sadly, despite concerted efforts, the Cassidys have never discovered the identity of this mystery singer.

As well as performing regularly at weddings and bar mitzvahs with a Top 40 band, Hugh was constantly seeking to improve the craftsmanship of the family trio of Eva's guitar, Dan's violin and himself on mandolin or electric bass guitar, and once he'd achieved his goal of becoming a champion power lifter he set his mind to securing a breakthrough for the fledgling family band. They practised regularly, but the children found it hard to deal with their demanding father. Hugh criticised Eva's vocals, which frustrated her. "Although Hugh only critiqued Eva's singing at this time he would often offer very helpful guidance to raise her level of music making," says Dan. "He stimulated Eva a lot in learning the Paul Simon tune 'American Tune' that he introduced her to."

Their first ever performance at the Fleet Reserve Club began disastrously. Eva was mortified by the falling microphone and began to cry. This awkward start became a bad omen: Eva would struggle with performing for the rest of her life.

Hugh took the band to several prestigious local venues. They entertained guests in the lobby of expensive five-star hotels, including the Hilton in Bethesda, and occasionally they performed at weddings, but Eva was too modest to feel at ease performing in front of the well-to-do. Their rendering of 'Too Young' by Nat King Cole was a case of life imitating art; the children were too callow to take on the pressures of regular gigs. Once this dawned on Hugh, he decided not to push his children to play in public with him any more.

After the demise of the trio, Dan turned his hand to the electric bass guitar, which made it easier for him to play with other musicians. Hugh taught him to play it and Dan, unlike Eva, was happy to accept his father's criticism. Eventually Hugh agreed to Dan and Eva playing together and advised them to look for musicians of their own age. This was no simple task: Dan and Eva had very few friends between them.

In 1976 Dan spent several days in Prince George's Hospital, Cheverly, following a leg operation. Eva would visit and, to pass the time, she brought along his violin and her guitar. Dan hadn't played for several days, but they tuned up and began to pick out a melody. They were immediately surprised and overjoyed by the quality of sound they produced together.

They built up their repertoire every day. One of their successes was 'Dust In The Wind' by Kansas, and they were big fans of Simon & Garfunkel. Their confidence in each other and their playing grew. Like Karen and Richard Carpenter, it appeared that Dan and Eva could look forward to a musical future as performing siblings.

Chapter 4

She'll Be Coming Round The Mountain

Eva was in danger of alienating her schoolmates; she had no interest whatsoever in sports or fashionable clothing. Music was the only thing that broke through Eva's social isolation. She practised frequently with Dan and her father, and she listened to her favourite albums for hours on end. Her musical talent had been ripening gradually.

The relationship between Dan and Eva was always excellent; the two shared a good ear for music and they developed a keen musical telepathy. Playing with Hugh was more complicated. She owed her father a lot and her musical tastes had been shaped by him, but she couldn't cope with his often tactless critical remarks. She knew he was probably right more often than not, but for a talented child moving towards the sensitive adolescent years it was better to keep some distance from a father who seemed to have projected all his hopes and dreams on to her.

When Dan and Eva moved on from junior high to Bowie High School in 1979 it was as if the sun began to shine again. In Bowie, it turned out they were in the midst of an entire generation of promising musicians, although it would take time to find them, withdrawn as they were. Eventually their occasional performances in front of school audiences brought Dan and Eva to their attention and they were invited to join a hard-rock band that specialised in heavy metal played by groups like Black Sabbath. Eva wasn't particularly a fan of this type of music, but she saw it as an opportunity to improve her voice and to play in a band where her father was not the dominant force. The uncompromising style of the music was also a way of countering Hugh's influence.

During this period Eva developed an attraction for dejected-looking boys dressed in black leather clothes who tried to camouflage their shyness with a prickly attitude. She began a relationship with a guy called Thurston that lasted for at least two years. A dominating character who rode a motorbike, Thurston was also a musician who sometimes played in the band. Dan liked him, Ruth and Celia couldn't stand him, and Hugh and Barbara believed Thurston to be anything but a positive influence on their youngest daughter. When Eva came to the same conclusion she broke off the relationship.

Eva's negative self-image continued to show itself in her art. When her brother discovered a drawing of a bleeding pig in Eva's bedroom and asked what she wanted to say with this work she answered, "This is me." She struggled with her appearance, believing herself to be overweight, although she never seriously tried to diet. Photos of Eva during adolescence portray her mood swings: some show her looking very melancholy indeed, but in others she is beautiful and happy.

The fledgling hard-rock band christened themselves Nightwing and took to the stage, sharing the bill at the Coffee House, and with three other bands in a series of concerts put on at Bowie High. Despite the mediocre sound system bought on a students' income, they started to attract attention. The audience was especially impressed by the calibre of the unknown lead singer. Although Eva didn't have any strong affinity with heavy metal, she had no difficulty creating the dramatic screaming howl that characterises the genre. Dan's violin added to the goth-like nature of the music. Though the band gave the siblings their first opportunity to hone their band skills, they struggled to rise above the volume of the other players.

Brother and sister Cassidy used the time between Sabbath-inspired rock sets to show the audience what they were capable of as a duo.

Years of crafting their art at home had resulted in a complete set list of impressive duets, all of which contrasted sharply with Nightwing's style. Those who saw them perform together remember these mini-concerts as if they were yesterday. Piano player and schoolmate Ned Judy, by far the best musician in the neighbourhood, sensed immediately that he had stumbled across something very special. He invited Dan and Eva to a rehearsal of his own band where they played 'Georgia On My Mind' by Hoagy Carmichael and 'Dog & Butterfly', a slow piece by the Canadian band Heart fronted by the Wilson sisters, Ann and Nancy. They also played Kansas' 'Dust In The Wind', Dan's violin picking out a magnificent melody above Eva's voice. It was clear to Ned that he had discovered something unique in Eva, that she stood out among other singers from Bowie. She possessed real quality and, compared with other female singers who had trouble with heavy material, exhibited self-restraint beyond her years. Ned decided there and then to work with her.

Ned Judy was a member of a band called Chaser, which played primarily Led Zeppelin and Kansas covers. But he had high hopes of starting a group that would concentrate on adventurous progressive rock with vocal harmonies. Dan and Eva would be perfect for what he had in mind.

They would join guitarist David Lourim, later to change his name to David Christopher because of a break down in his relationship with his father. David was already friendly with Dan and Eva as he and Dan were in the same class at school and their musical paths had crossed once before when they performed in the school hall after which fellow pupils, swept up by the fun, threw coins in their direction in a show of admiration. The teenagers had talked in the past about starting a band that would play only "good" music. David was a fan of Eva's too and he was struck by the likeness of her voice to Heart's lead singer, Ann Wilson.

Drummer Mark Merella was an easy-going guy whose parents worked for the government in Washington, D.C. They thought it important that their son develop musically so they helped him as much as they could, allowing him to use their garage as a music space which would "keep him from hanging around in the street". Eva would have a short, not particularly serious relationship with Mark that lasted for about a year.

Bass player Larry Melton, who had played in a fusion band that covered the music of Jeff Beck, rounded off the group. Since the Cassidy children had in the past found it hard to mix with new people, it was something of a miracle that this bunch fitted together as well as they did. In fact, even today most of the original line-up still play in a jazz band called Mosaic.

There were two important conditions that needed to be met before Dan and Eva would agree to join the new band: that their musical ideas be shared by the other members and, since they found it so difficult to adapt to new situations, that they clicked on a personal level. After they agreed to attend a rehearsal, Ned drove Dan and Eva from school to the studio and was surprised that they didn't say a word during the entire journey. However, this first rehearsal – in 1980 – proved to be the beginning of a long and very close friendship.

Soon the band took to practising every evening, even if one of the members was absent. The boys treated Eva as an equal and were never arrogant or brash towards her. Musical growth was a goal, but the joy of being together with close friends was just as important to them. They referred to themselves as "collective hermits" – they had finally found their creative counterparts in a high school dominated by jocks. Eva's confidence began to grow in a group where she finally felt accepted.

The group's name, Stonehenge, originated from an earlier collaboration between Dan, David and Mark. In the summer of 1980 Eva, Dan and Dave Lourim had teamed up with a singer named Ed 'Roach' Silverman, an extrovert character who liked to sing Queen songs and wear a tutu. They called their band Blue Wind but it was a short-lived affair, lasting for just one gig. It was after this that Dave and Dan started the trio with Mark Merella that they called Stonehenge, after a poster of the prehistoric English monument on Mark's wall, and they retained the name for their new band.

The raucous rehearsals in the Merella garage could be heard all over the neighbourhood and it didn't take long before the first curious visitors found their way to them. Soon enough the garage had transformed into a venue that attracted the ostracised youth of Bowie. Both sexes were inspired to seek out Stonehenge, which meant that Eva could finally share her love of music with other girls.

Outside of the Bowie High Coffee House, Stonehenge didn't often perform in public. Their repertoire didn't lend itself to dancing, the pieces were often too long and the music was too esoteric for a young party audience. However, one of Eva's specialities was to imitate other female singers, and this often entranced the crowds. Even better than her impression of Ann Wilson from Heart was her notoriously abandoned Janis Joplin impersonation, specifically 'Turtle Blues', a fast-paced blues song with a rock-like cadence, that brought audiences into a state approaching ecstasy. No one would have expected this inconspicuous girl to belt out such a difficult song so well: it was as though she poured all of her suppressed emotion into the performance.

Joplin could not have been more different from Eva; she had been a heavy-drinking stage animal, a man-eating rock bitch and a coarse language-using junkie. However, Joplin's often crazed behaviour was born out of loneliness and lack of self-worth. She was shunned by the dull mediocrity, much the same as Eva was. Whereas Eva dealt with this by avoiding the limelight, Janis Joplin craved attention and made sure she got it.

'Turtle Blues' was a showcase for Eva, but the boys enjoyed performing one particularly complex piece. Despite their various musical backgrounds, the band members shared a liking for British prog rock behemoths Yes. 'Close To The Edge', a monumental four-part symphony from their album of the same name, is over 18 minutes long. The boys learnt the entire piece by heart, improvising large parts as they went along.

While the band members were united in their love of progressive rock, Stonehenge came to mean much more to them than just music. The boys and Eva began to spend every spare moment with each other, going to the movies, building campfires and organising weekend trips away. They camped in the mountains, and walked and cycled in the woods, taking full advantage of their proximity to one of the USA's most stunning national parks. In the heart of Virginia, an area of outstanding natural beauty, Shenandoah is a long and narrow park bound by the Shenandoah River and Valley on the west side and the impressive hills of the Virginia Piedmont on the east. Camping is a popular pastime in these hills, where bears and snakes are not an uncommon sight.

Another popular destination was the Merellas' beach house in Ocean City, a seaside resort on the opposite side to Chesapeake Bay. Eva and Dan brought their instruments along, and with their newfound confidence, they performed on the boardwalk to an admiring public who stopped their leisurely walks to crowd round the duo. Finally, several policemen had to intervene to break up the temporary gathering.

It began to dawn on this merry band of musicians that they were too good to play for only a handful of half-drunk schoolmates in the Merella garage, and Dan in particular was keen to capitalise on their musical talent. They discovered that there was a thriving industry based around recruiting performers for business gatherings, weddings and parties in Washington, D.C. The boys purchased suitable clothing and visited an agent. On August 12, 1981 they signed a contract with one of the capital's talent agencies.

Realising that their experimental progressive rock was unlikely to go down well at weddings, they pored over Hugh's old American songbooks and started rehearsing standards like 'Misty', 'Autumn Leaves', 'Mack The Knife', 'Secret Love' and other jazz, rock and blues favourites. The group needed a change of name to reflect this new musical direction, so they called themselves Easy Street in reference to how easy it had been to get on the road and earn money as a gigging band. It was at this point that Mark Merella quit the band, the American Songbook a leap too far for his musical tastes, and he was replaced with drummer John Perrault.

The group also had to consider their image for the first time. The boys took to performing in showy blue tuxedos with Eva in a flattering black dress, which wasn't to her liking. As ever she hated to look girly and would later confess to her mother that she had once secretly destroyed a pink blouse bought for her.

Easy Street's first performance was at the Manassas Lodge of the Elks Association, a fraternity in Manassas, Virginia, on September 19, 1981.

Eva didn't sing in every song and – modest as she was – she left the stage to give the boys the chance to excel on the instrumentals. During one such break, she was invited to dance by an older gentleman. She was too stunned to refuse, but this was the first and last time she let such an incident occur, and from then on she remained glued to the stage.

Easy Street jumped without a safety net. Performing to large, sometimes paying, audiences was something else. They encountered new and often unexpected situations and gigging became a crash course in adaptability. They also found themselves going from performing in front of well-behaved audiences to others that were often worse for wear for alcohol.

Eva found these gigs particularly uncomfortable. Not only were drunken requests bellowed from the floor a hindrance, but American audiences on a night out when partying is the prime motivation can be hard to impress. A culture of watching, rather than listening, pervades and music is often expected merely to entertain, as opposed to create a genuine connection. Ned Judy: "They want musicians to jump up and down in coloured costumes. Americans have no patience. Even civilised and cultivated spectators lack the concentration to listen carefully." Eva was advised by those who saw her not to look so serious on stage: "Make sure the audience feels good when they return home. Give them a good time, make jokes," she was told.

The rest of the band got to see Eva's fun side too. She had a keen sense of humour and an eye for the ridiculous side of life, and after shows they would discuss their strange experiences and roar with laughter. But Eva had no desire to come over as a giggly girl onstage. She regarded singing and music-making as serious art forms. The execution of a song was the representation of deeply held emotions and she simply couldn't be light-hearted towards something of such importance.

Eva experimented with pot and alcohol along with her fellow musicians, but the partying never really got a grip on her, since her dislike for exhibitionism was greater than her desire to forget her troubles. "It would have been better for her if she had lived less frenetically," her former band members conclude. "A more easy-going attitude would have made her life more pleasant." Sometimes Eva tossed down a glass of Canadian Mist, after which she might crawl out of her shell and experience ultimate freedom onstage.

The band was offered two gigs over Christmas 1981 and, true to their nonconformist and enthusiastic character, they signed up for both. They didn't have to travel far, performing on Christmas and Boxing Day at the Market Inn in their hometown. Christmas gigs can be tricky – bars can be the haunt of those who are alone during the festive period, drowning their sorrows in dark corners. In fact, Eva's serious presentation fitted the mood perfectly and her songs had a comforting effect. That night the air at the Market Inn was blue with smoke, making it difficult to see the stage. Easy Street's family and friends came to watch them, all bar Eva's father, Hugh, who seldom showed up at her performances, something that constantly surprised those around his daughter.

The band opened with several Christmas songs, including 'Silent Night', 'O Come All Ye Faithful' and a gospel shuffle-style version of 'Go Tell It On The Mountain'. Eva would continue to find solace in Christmas carols, and went on to record two songs which appeared on Chuck Brown's *The Spirit Of Christmas* in 1999.

Easy Street was formed as a commercial proposition, to earn money, albeit not a great deal, but Stonehenge had been a basis for friendship, a shared sense of musical values and the development of an attitude to life. The two groups existed simultaneously, the band members spoke the same language and their bond grew ever closer. Stonehenge had a cult following locally because they were such skilled musicians and played music that other bands were unable to play. After playing a handful of Bowie gigs, they performed two big concerts at PG Community College. David Lourim was the first to quit, leaving after a year to pursue his love of hard rock with another band, and he was replaced by an equally adept guitarist, Todd Bauchspies.

The new line-up practised so often they appeared to become squatters in the Merella garage where they continued to rehearse, Mark Merella still being a friend and a member of Stonehenge. They began to incorporate voice-specific practice, developing a real taste for creating complex harmonies and taking the melodic four-part harmonies of Crosby, Stills, Nash & Young as their inspiration. It was here that Eva really impressed, patiently passing on her innate knowledge of part-singing to her fellow band members.

It was only a matter of time before they began to write their own songs. There were no egos in the band and Eva felt more and more at ease with the boys, trusting them implicitly. There were still moments where she worked away from the group in total silence on her pen and ink drawings and paintings, but this in itself was a sign of trust. Eva had never been able to create art in the company of others, so this was a major step forward for the shy teenager. The boys recognised her talents and encouraged her to improve her work.

Eva had not given up on the idea of a career in the arts, but she was also still extremely self-critical. When she was dissatisfied with a drawing she would destroy it in a dramatic flourish, throwing the remains into the nearest wastepaper basket. To the boys, saving these drawings became a sport. Ned Judy built up a unique art collection in this way. Eva was in good company: William Shakespeare, the Bard himself, discarded *Romeo And Juliet* and *The Merchant Of Venice* after they were debuted by the playing company the Lord Chamberlain's Men, regarding the plays as "working material". His friends rescued the scripts, guaranteeing audience enjoyment and critical plaudits into modern times.

Eva woke early every day. She had found a job as a 'hot walker' at a racecourse just outside Bowie, and was required to handle enormous, highly-strung thoroughbreds after training, cooling them down and returning them to their stalls. Eva was short but strong and, astonishingly, she proved very capable of dealing with these large animals. But it could be a dangerous job: Eva once showed Ned a set of large teeth marks on her shoulder from one temperamental filly; luckily she had been wearing a heavy leather jacket.

Eva was enchanted by the animals to the extent that she was traumatised when one horse managed to escape. During a stroll she and the horse met a brightly coloured children's tricycle which caused the animal to rear up on its hind legs, ripping the reins out from her hands and escaping.

Happily, such occurrences were few and far between. Unsurprisingly,

Eva had more difficulties with her colleagues. One of the horse trainers was an older gentleman who drove a long Cadillac. Eva was enlisted to drive him to work in the vehicle, but she came close to damaging the expensive car when she slammed on the breaks to avoid a squirrel in the road. This empathy for animals saw her involved in another awkward situation after she complained about the rat traps in the stables, and from that moment on she became a laughing stock. She hit rock bottom when a fellow worker caught a rat, torturing and killing it in front of her in the most brutal way possible. It was too much for Eva: she quit her job, concluding that even those who worked with animals could hate them. Her next job was at Behnke's Garden Nursery, where her mother, Barbara, worked several hours a week. Her work there reinvigorated her love of nature and the outdoors and she discovered that she liked working with plants and trees. She wasn't afraid of getting her hands dirty and didn't mind lifting heavy pots.

In the run-up to the long summer months of 1982, the Bowie musicians were looking for a more profitable way to utilise their talents. Wild World amusement park in Largo had opened its doors in 1981, adding several new rides and fairground attractions and retaining some of the safari elements of its former animal-park heritage. The park staged several different musical shows and they were always on the lookout for musicians. In its opening year Dan, Todd and Mark and a new bass player, Danny Powell, played in a country jamboree six days a week. Larry and Ned also joined a Broadway adaptation staged in one of Wild World's amphitheatres, performing seven shows a week throughout the three-month summer holiday. In 1983, Larry and Ned were promoted to seats in a revue show's orchestra pit while Dan joined a country spectacle.

Eva was too restrained for such an informal, cheerful atmosphere and she had no desire to sing country songs. However, in 1983 her friends persuaded her to attend an audition at Wild World and she was a hit. She left her job at Behnke's, although she would continue to return there from time to time.

The days at Wild World were long and the working conditions were miserable but sometimes there were unexpected moments of relief and joy. On one occasion, the band was obscured by a wandering group of llamas that made their way slowly past the stage, causing much excitement and laughter.

For Eva and her friends, playing in the park proved an excellent opportunity to work on their craft in front of an uncritical audience. They gained a wealth of experience in discipline and performance, much like The Beatles had during their marathon sets in Hamburg. Wild World also provided the musicians with a regular income. Larry and Ned bought a four-track recorder from their first wage packet. Eva would spend many hours, and often whole days, in Ned's small home studio. Experimenting in the studio was the perfect outlet for Eva. She continued to hone her fabulous capacity for spontaneously singing several parts and never writing them down. To Ned she said, "I see the song lines before me, like colour patterns."

Eva made the most of the four tracks, building up layers, delays and dubbing more parts in. She loved to play with sounds and she recorded all kinds of stories and ambient noises, as well as various audio holiday greetings for her friends. During this time, she began to develop her classic arrangement of 'Over The Rainbow'. It took her years to perfect it.

Eva and Larry recorded the song 'Do Lord' together in his room. It was a complicated tune with a multi-part *a cappella* gospel chorus and rhythmical hand clapping, and it would later be used for her *Time After Time* album, released in 2000 on the Blix Street label under the title 'Way Beyond The Blue'. Larry was saddened by this experience: "If they had called me I would have been able to alter a few things. This was the work of two naïve people in their twenties, recorded in a spare moment. It is clear that Blix Street wanted to release some material in a high tempo. They also used some of my photographs without mentioning me. The whole album was made in a hurry."

Eva's childlike recordings took on a greater seriousness after she met singer and composer Michael Ingram at Wild World amusement park during the summer of 1983. Ingram was stage-managing the main stage song-and-dance spectacular *Music, Music, Music*. Eva was pickin' and grinnin' in the country band just down the walkway past the lemonade and corn dogs.

Ingram, fresh from a year of film school at UCLA, was idealistic but starving, but now he found himself in a real job making real money, and to top it off he was surrounded by more talent than he had found in Los Angeles. He made friends with many of the musicians, singers and dancers, and really clicked with Ned Judy, Larry Melton and Eva. Ned and Michael worked especially well together. Ned turned Michael's lyrics and ideas into fully realised songs and Eva made them shine.

After the summer Michael travelled to Ohio to finish college at Kent State, and over the next few years he would return to Maryland where he stayed with Ned. They recorded songs in Ned's bedroom, and Ned discovered a talent for transforming Michael's lyrics into a real song within a few hours. They would then enlist Larry to add some interesting bass lines and finally Eva would arrive. She'd pick up the lyric sheet, sing it through a few times with Ned accompanying her, and then sit by the microphone with Ned manning the four-track cassette recorder, and create something quite special.

Michael Ingram left to travel around Europe, staying in New York for a while on his return, and arrived back in Maryland in the eighties. His plan was to make a record with his old friends and try to sell it to an independent British music label. They recorded several songs under the name Characters Without Names. Ingram sent several copies to a string of record companies, but only Mute Records responded, saying: "The girl has a pretty good voice, but I don't know what I could do with the songs. Call me when you play out and I'll come by to see the show."

Ingram decided to get a place in Baltimore with Ned so they could work on new material. They had a great downtown loft with plenty of room to record. They wrote songs with a theatrical character; nothing was strange and anything seemed possible. Their ambition was to present their completed work in a multimedia show alongside projections of Eva's artwork. Regrettably, none of this ever happened.

During this period, the band members held down various regular jobs: Larry was employed at the guitar factory Paul Reed Smith, Ned played in a Top 40 covers band and Michael worked on a fruit and nuts stand. They all saw it as a very creative time and practised their music while looking for a break.

Eva would polish her songs over and over again and her voice and guitar playing developed quickly as a result. She was still entranced by black jazz and soul singers, Ella Fitzgerald, Aretha Franklin, Ray Charles and Stevie Wonder, whose music she found richer than the four-part harmonies of Crosby, Stills, Nash & Young. Ella Fitzgerald in particular opened up a new musical world for the teenager. Slowly but surely jazz music crawled under Eva's pale skin and she was soon able to imitate Fitzgerald's highly technical scats.

Together with Ned, Eva began attending concerts to see and hear black artists. They saw Ella Fitzgerald at Wolf Trap, a cultural centre several miles west of Washington, D.C., and Ray Charles and Aretha Franklin at Constitution Hall. Eva incorporated all these influences into her playing, bringing originality to her blossoming style by looking for connections between her voice and the guitar. She began to discover that she created her best work alone, yet her fear of the spotlight kept her from capitalising on this.

Even in the studio she tried to hide herself. Her predilection for layering her voice with echo was notorious, despite assurances that she was at her best without such manipulation. Nobody could sing as purely and perfectly as Eva, but she had an innate desire to obscure the truth with microphone settings meant for talent lesser than her own. Eva was also afraid of stripped-down guitar playing and she draped all her recordings in a bed of keyboard-synthesised violins, relying on them far too heavily. Onstage she looked for safety in the cushion of her fellow musicians.

Eva also continued to hedge her bets. Thanks to the recording equipment available to her she was in an almost constant musical flow, but she still wanted to develop her art work. Painting, drawing and making her own beads and necklaces grew more and more important to her. She made a scale replica of a black bear for Ned, which was so huge he had to store it at his parents' home.

She painted a portrait of Ned for his 19th birthday. Both of them loved the outdoors, and she positioned him at his grand piano between two enormous mountains. Two elements were typical of Eva's gift – her preference for the colours blue and white and the fact that she didn't finish the painting.

The painting still hangs on the wall in Ned's music room. It had clearly come from the heart and when Eva presented it to Ned, he suddenly realised how much their friendship meant. Their romantic relationship blossomed the same day and appeared strong. They lived in the moment, never speaking about the future, but sometimes Eva would express her wish to "take care of a little Eva" one day.

Chapter 5

Pimps And Players

The seemingly eternal summer of friendship and love couldn't last forever. Always restless, Michael Ingram convinced some of his friends to travel to Los Angeles. Ned, Larry and saxophone player Mark Izzi saw the limitations of making music in Maryland and made the move to study at the Musical Institute in Hollywood, although Michael was the only one who would stay in California longer than a couple of years. Dan went to stay with family in Germany in 1984 in an attempt to perform in Europe, joining a folk band as their fiddler.

Eva didn't know what to do. She sent material to the Californian Institute of the Arts in Valencia and they replied by saying she would be welcome to enrol. But relocating was simply a bridge too far for her. Eva lacked an adventurous or enterprising nature, which she shared with her sister, Margret, who seldom left the United States. She didn't like the idea of having to settle somewhere else. It had taken long enough to find a safe group of friends in Bowie.

Furthermore, the institute bore the stamp of Walt Disney, who had founded and created it in the sixties. This bothered Eva, since she was used to working freely and making her own creative decisions. She had always found it difficult when teachers tried to alter her technique, even if they did so cautiously, an attitude that lingered from her youth and the laborious manner in which she and her father communicated. As a little girl she had followed him blindly, but from adolescence she had tried to move away from her dominant father, albeit with scant success. Her father's voice had finally become the voice of her own conscience. She couldn't live without him, but she needed and craved independence.

CalArts would also be expensive: she would have to pay a deposit on registration, plus $13,000 a year in school fees. Eva didn't even have a bank account, and she would have been reliant on her father to provide the fees. Typically, she neither mentioned the issue to him, nor arranged to pay it herself. The registration date quietly slipped by.

Weeks later Eva informed Barbara that the prestigious Disney academy had accepted her, but that it was too late to take proper action. Barbara completely understood her daughter's explanation, but the ambitious Hugh was furious. "I didn't want you to pay all that money for me," Eva maintained. "I would have preferred to take that decision," responded Hugh. Larry and Ned asked Eva to come to LA to perform with them, but she couldn't bring herself to go.

Deep in her heart Barbara was glad that Eva had chosen to stay at home, especially since Dan had left for Europe. She and Eva still spent every Sunday together, visiting museums and galleries, going to antique stores and collecting stones and shells. Barbara was also happy that Eva wanted to stretch her artistic wings beyond the restrictions of Walt Disney cartoons. She convinced her daughter to register for drawing classes at Prince George's Community College in Largo, which was much closer to home and a lot cheaper.

During her time at the academy she was awarded the Blue Ribbon prize, an annual accolade given by the art department at Prince George's Community College, for one of her oil paintings. This early portrait shows a New Guinea chief with an impressive face. It is easy to spot Eva's sparkle in the painting, manifested in the cigarette held between the native Indonesian's fingers.

The black lady she painted in a similar style in the same period isn't smiling, nor is she sad. She looks away, but not shyly, and wears a large blue cap on her head, showing her pride and independence. Eva also made a silkscreen from a portrait of jazz trumpeter Miles Davis and printed the image on T-shirts, which she sold. Most of the time, though, she simply gave her artwork away.

However well she was doing, Eva couldn't help but feel trapped during her art lessons at Prince George's. No teacher would have been able to stimulate Eva because she was so headstrong in her creative impulses: she knew exactly what she wanted and what she didn't and she didn't accept any interference. She stayed only one semester at the school.

Nearly all of Eva's musician friends had moved to Los Angeles, but David Lourim had remained nearby. He had left Stonehenge because of musical differences, but he retained pleasant memories of Eva's voice and versatile musical talents. David spent his days composing and recording music, working professionally with a 24-track recorder on a project he named 'Method Actor'. He liked to experiment with all kinds of sounds and 24 tracks gave him the chance to enjoy his musical freedom to the full. He played most of the instruments himself, but would sometimes invite friends to join him. Soon enough he looked to Eva for inspiration.

David didn't adapt his music to Eva's voice because he knew she was able to sing anything. They worked from improvisation: he didn't write down her parts and she would listen to new fragments, filling them with her vocals any way she liked. It was the perfect way to use Eva's talents. David gave her all the time she needed and he didn't criticise her. Eva not only invented the lead parts, but she created harmonies for second, third and sometimes fourth parts on the spot. They took their time, working for several years and crafting something beautiful.

David and Eva were delighted with the results and they tried to interest record companies. After they had built up enough material, David started to organise matters in an effort to put themselves on the map. They enlisted other musicians for their live performances, including bassist Ken Fiester and drummer Jim Campbell, and additional musicians Ned Judy on piano, Bob Fiester on guitar, Jeff Lourim on synthesisers, Tom Crawford and Mark Izzi on saxophones and Tom Prasada-Rao on violin.

In 1986 Method Actor played several times at The Bayou, a live music club in Georgetown which had been a stop-off for artists such as U2 and Bruce Springsteen on their earliest US tours. The owner was impressed by their melodious rock music. The following year he organised a talent show for his fledgling bands and invited big shots from the record industry, including reps from Warner Music. Eva took to the stage dressed in hippie attire, while the rest of the group paraded the typical eighties style.

During the show they became aware of the Warner VIPs in the balcony. Knowing she was being judged, Eva found it hard to sing, and the rest of the group were also paralysed with fear. Their performance was a disaster. Halfway through the show the executives got up and left for the bar.

Next on the bill was The Judybats, a band from Knoxville, Tennessee. They gave an excellent show, convincing the guys from Warner Brothers who had returned with their refreshments. The Judybats signed a record contract that very afternoon. David and his friends were bitterly disappointed but they were surprised to discover that Eva reacted with relief. She was afraid that she would be imprisoned in a musical style that wasn't entirely her own. She enjoyed playing the music of Method Actor, but she needed more freedom. Fear of commitment would become the leitmotif of Eva's musical career.

Anita Court is a narrow cul-de-sac with old, white houses in the town of Rockville. At the rear of number five is the entrance to a cellar where Chris Biondo had taken over Tom Scott's recording facility, Black Pond Studio. Chris would become a major influence in Eva Cassidy's life and musical career.

In the spring of 1987 Chris worked with the guys from the Method Actor project, but he was missing a female voice on the recordings. "Didn't I tell you?" David said. "Eva will be here any minute." They waited, but she didn't turn up. Chris decided to look for her, and when he opened the back door there was Eva, shielded by a black cowboy hat. She was too afraid to enter. "Get in," Chris commanded. "I don't have all day."

Once everyone was settled, Chris began to explain how the session would work, but David interrupted: "Eva knows exactly what to do."

He was right: Chris was blown away by Eva's powerful voice and he was especially impressed with her ability to improvise three- and four-part harmonies. Despite her admiring audience, Eva preferred to sing her parts from the broom cupboard where nobody could see her.

The album *Method Actor* was released in 1988, on both vinyl and cassette. It was intended as a showcase for David Christopher's composing, arranging and playing, but Eva's voice was prominent. She sang lead vocals on eight of the songs and also contributed most of the background vocals.

The album cover was especially eye-catching. Eva had created a collage that brought together a mixture of fantasy and historical characters, among them Anne Frank, the young Jewish diarist who had spent most of the Second World War hiding from the Nazis with her family in an Amsterdam attic before being betrayed in the final year of the conflict. Her story resonated firmly with Eva. On the back of the album cover were the names of the most important contributors, including Eva, producer David Lourim, bass player Ken Fiester, drummer Jim Campbell, pianist Ned Judy, guitarist Bob Fiester, keyboard player Jeff Lourim, saxophonists Tom Crawford and Mark Izzi and violinist Tom Prasada-Rao. Chris Biondo is listed as sound engineer. The A-side was called 'This Side', the B-side 'That Side'.

Pop music wasn't really Eva's thing, but she was very proud of her first record, handing it out generously to her friends and acquaintances. She seemed to be more proud of the cover, which was completely her own work, than of the actual record, asking her friends what they thought of the drawing rather than the songs.

Eva had plenty of experience recording on a four-track, but making a real record in a genuine studio was a giant leap forward in her career. It was reviewed in the Weekend section of *The Washington Post* on September 2, 1988: "Eva Cassidy is the noteworthy singer fronting this Gaithersburg quartet. She also did the strikingly eccentric etchings on the cover. Cassidy's got a cool, otherworldly tone on songs like 'Look Into My Eyes' and when she multi-tracks her vocals she sounds like Heart's Ann Wilson minus the histrionics; there's a faintly metallic Grace Slick tinge in the neo psychedelic 'How Will It End'. The band, led by David Lourim, who writes the songs, plays the fluid guitar lines and adds the washes of keyboards, creates sometimes dreamy, sometimes playful backdrops. Another find."

When Method Actor decided to take their album on the road they had to seek out more musicians to reproduce the sound in a live format. Tony and Marybeth Bernui were friends of David and he asked them to replicate Eva's background vocals to free her for lead. This was easier said than done. To begin with, Eva hadn't written down any of her parts, since all of her harmonies had been invented on the spot. She always sang by heart and often improvised. Tony and Marybeth did their best to learn the vocals by listening to the record endlessly, but they weren't able to catch the right lines. What appeared to be simple actually turned out to be fairly complicated and Eva had to explain every line in turn. The backing singers quickly realised that not only was Eva a very special singer, she was also an extremely talented composer, arranger and producer.

Tony and Marybeth's admiration increased when they got onstage with Eva. They thought it remarkable that she was so insecure about her own abilities, despite her tremendous talents. Unusually, Eva wanted her backing singers right next to her because she was afraid to be in the spotlight on her own.

During Dan's brief stay in the US, Hugh took Dan and Eva to a concert by Alison Krauss at the Birchmere. Much impressed with her singing and fiddle playing, Eva and Dan went to see her on several more occasions. Indeed, Illinois-born Alison Krauss would become a huge influence on Eva, who for years listened to her recordings over and over again in her truck as she drove to and from work.

Several months passed and Eva and Chris Biondo lost track of each other, but to his great surprise she eventually got back in touch to say she hadn't given up on the idea of starting a musical career of her own. Although she was obliged to remain there for financial reasons, she wanted to quit her job at Behnke's and was looking for studio work.

In order to attract attention she needed a demo tape, which she asked Chris to arrange for her. Studio time was expensive, but since Chris liked Eva he asked her to draw a portrait of his dog, Bernice, as a form of payment. Chris had discovered Bernice in a local veterinary hospital called Montgomery Animal Hospital, where she had been left for almost a year. Evidently staff from the Russian Embassy in Washington D.C. had brought her there to run some research tests but never picked her up again. Eternally sympathetic to members of the animal kingdom, on the bottom of her painting Eva wrote: "She represents all that is good and kind in the world."

Chris and Eva made an odd pairing – it was hardly possible to find a greater difference between two people. Chris was outspoken, extroverted, quick and decisive while Eva was withdrawn, introverted and cautious. Chris was used to the presence of headstrong musicians and he could be very blunt, which of course intimidated Eva.

But they also had much in common – their love of music, a particular sense of humour and their appreciation of life in general. Eva felt safe in Chris' presence and he lost his armour when she was in his studio. Chris discovered Eva's love for animals in an unusual way: when a large group of ants invaded the studio floor, Chris wanted to know the best way to get rid of them. "Why don't you get a paper plate, put some honey on it, let them walk onto it and take them to the woods?"

Eva visited Chris' studio on a regular basis. The friendship between the two deepened and Chris' respect for her musical abilities grew. Chris had started rock band She's Melting with his ex-wife, Christine, and the singer Yvonne Charbonneau, his brother's girlfriend. Yvonne would soon have a special Eva Cassidy work of art: a tattoo on her ankle that Eva designed for her. Jim Campbell and Doug Casteen finished the line-up. Eva was asked to sing background vocals for the band, but it was a short-lived project and they performed only once at The Bayou.

Chris introduced Eva to other studios and she was soon earning money for her back-up singing. Working with Eva was easy: she could harmonise, her pitch was good, her synchronisation was fine and her musical memory was excellent. She understood completely what musicians needed and she could fit into any role. Experience Unlimited (or E.U.) was a Washington-based go-go and rhythm and blues crew who were looking for a female gospel choir for their 1989 album *Living Large*. Through multitracked recording, Eva fulfilled the role of an entire choir on her own.

She even tried her hand at rap. Chris' studio was used by rappers who could be very rough and tough, but Eva had a strangely disarming effect on them. Californian rapper Earl Stevens, better known as E-40, employed her help on the 1996 release *Tha Hall Of Game*. Chris recorded the atypical Eva-lyrics: "I wanna thank you pimps and players for sharing this with me/ I wanna thank you all of the hustlers for showing me your life on the street." She sang these lines without blinking and the record was a success. In time Eva's voice would even find its way on to a track by world famous hip-hop artist Tupac Shakur, although the recording was never released.

Chris thought it would be interesting to create a completely new band centred around Eva's prodigious musical talent, and asked his neighbour and friend Mike Dove for help. Mike worked as a guitar repairman in a music shop and knew an impressive network of local musicians. He met Eva in his back garden, which was attached to Chris' basement studio.

Mike listened to the tapes Chris and Eva had made and immediately came up with the name of Keith Grimes as a potential collaborator. He knew Keith had played in a band called The Barflies and that this band had recently broken up. Keith's guitar playing had the exact subtlety and refinement Eva's voice needed.

Chris knew Keith because they had once lived in the same building, Keith in the apartment below Chris', and he called him to the studio immediately. "I have a tape of a singer I am working with," he said. "You have to listen to this singer – she is really great." Keith's immediate reaction was downbeat. He had developed a healthy dose of scepticism after years of promises of fabulous singers who later turned out to be mediocre. Despite his concerns, he decided to make the drive to Chris' studio, conjuring up myriad excuses to decline the offer en route.

On hearing the tape his scepticism melted away in an instant. In fact, he had to control his excitement: this was exactly the voice he had been looking for. "I'd really like to meet this singer and see if we can do something together," he said.

Chris decided to play bass himself. William "JuJu" House, drummer of Experience Unlimited, was willing to play the drums as a favour to Chris, his close friend, although the music wasn't really his scene. They also tried drummer Jim Campbell, but he had little time due to other musical obligations and he was more into rock than Eva's folk music. Kent Wood was drafted in to play keyboards, but he left soon after as his career took off.

Lenny Williams had been a bar pianist and had studied classical piano and jazz, before exploring rock'n'roll and rock music as a teenager. He was introduced to Chris Biondo by singer-songwriter Roger Henderson in 1987, the same year that he recorded some of his new songs in Chris' studio. On hearing 'Penny To My Name', Chris suggested Eva sing it. Although he admits that Eva did not make a huge first impression, she liked the song and they decided to record it, with Lenny on piano and Dan (who had returned from his travels in Europe for a visit) accompanying. It turned out to be one of the few songs of which Eva was the original performer.

Lenny seemed to be the perfect replacement for Kent Wood but he was unenthusiastic about joining the band. He certainly didn't underestimate Eva's qualities, but quality was something they took for granted. These excellent musicians were used to grafting in a music industry that seldom rewarded talent with success. Essentially, they didn't want to get their hopes up. Still, Chris was impressed and persuaded Lenny to join and a very reluctant Eva to call the group The Eva Cassidy Band. He suggested they hire a manager.

Al Dale was manager of several local bands in the eighties and a regular at the Anita Court studio. On one occasion he arrived to pick up some tapes just as Chris was recording with Eva. "Who the hell is that?" Al asked and he stayed a bit longer to listen to this incredible voice. After the recording Eva introduced herself to Al. "Are you the girl that was singing a few minutes ago?" Al asked and Eva nodded her head modestly. Al was shocked: he thought he had been listening to a black woman.

Several days later Al called Chris. "This girl is really great, she can have a great future in showbusiness." Chris agreed, but he made it clear that Eva didn't believe in her own potential. Al offered his help.

He started by working on her extreme shyness. She could also be stubborn, making it doubly difficult for Al to prise her away from her old self. Marketing would present another problem altogether; Eva liked to do a bit of everything, taking influences from many different genres and making them her own. However, the fact that she would never become a typical pop star didn't intimidate the manager – in fact, it was an advantage that Eva took herself seriously, since so many female artists in the pop industry used their femininity to degrading effect. Yet, she still despised the stage. "Let me make a few records and then you can sell them," she suggested. Despite her obvious talents, Eva had no desire for fame and was often heard to say: "I don't need to be famous. What I would like is to have a cottage at the oceanside, where I can make music and create art." This was ultimately far more important to her than fame and fortune.

Chapter 6

I Don't Think This Is Me

Rockville, a suburb on the north side of Washington, D.C., is at the core of the Interstate Technology Corridor, home to numerous software and biotechnology companies. It is also commemorated in the 1984 R.E.M. track 'Don't Go Back To Rockville'. Chris Biondo, son of an Italian father and American mother, grew up here and Eva would go on to perform in venues all over Rockville that have since been transformed into Chinese restaurants, English pubs, Brazilian barbecues and American pool halls. She also sang at several open-mic nights at Durty Nelly's in Bethesda, where she used a backing tape and where some members of the audience refused to believe that they were hearing a live voice.

The Eva Cassidy Band's first performance took place in March 1991 at Fatty's, an after-work bar not far from the Rockville Metro. Keith Grimes made a list of possible songs to cover onstage, but Eva often chose no more than four, electing instead to sing those that were important to her lyrically as well as musically. If she came with a song herself it was always a ballad. She was an excellent ballad singer, but her choice of repertoire was often too limited. The first set list went as follows: 'Take Me To The River', 'Nightbird', 'When The Whistle Blows', 'Drown In My Own Tears', 'San Francisco Bay Blues', 'As Lovely As You',

'Take My Breath Away', 'Respect', 'Stormy Monday', 'Down Home Blues', 'People Get Ready', 'Wishing Well', 'Do Right Woman', 'Angel', 'Drowning In A Sea Of Love', 'True Colors', 'Welcome To The Club' and 'Something's Got A Hold On Me'. Due to their limited repertoire they played some of the songs twice.

The group employed a sound man, but when they discovered he was earning more than all the members of the band put together, they decided to learn how to combine the installation of a mixing console with their playing. Eva bought a PA system for the band and from that moment on they controlled their own music.

They played all sorts of venues. They were regulars at the Trade Winds, a Chinese restaurant not far from the Congressional Plaza in Rockville, where they performed every Tuesday and were paid in delicious food. Eva and Keith Grimes duetted several times at The Wharf in Alexandria, on the south side of Washington, D.C., one of the few venues that featured them that is still in existence today.

Eva and Keith often recorded their music on cassette tapes, with and without the presence of a live audience. Despite their reputation as perfectionists, some of these home-made tapes were released after Eva's death, one of which, 'You Take My Breath Away', appearing on the 2003 album *American Tune*. They were still experimenting with some of the songs, so Keith didn't always know the exact chord changes; on 'You Take My Breath Away' he had clearly lost his way, and the sound engineers have tried to camouflage this on the album.

Keith was astonished that these recordings were ever released. Eva was very precise and she would have hated the idea of millions of people hearing material that was substandard. She was known for working for years on a single arrangement. Nevertheless, Keith would in due course hand over all his tapes to Bill Straw, the head of Blix Street Records, Eva's eventual record label.

Keith's influence on Eva was huge, especially in the beginning. Although Eva played a few solo electric guitar pieces with a white Fender Stratocaster on 'Over The Rainbow' and 'Ain't No Sunshine', Keith would normally play lead, while she was an excellent rhythm guitarist. Keith had a prowess for entertaining, which was something

Eva shunned completely. She could look very uncomfortable if he showed off by playing his guitar behind his head. In the main, though, Keith tried to adapt his playing to Eva's voice, playing his guitar parts softer than he was used to. Looking back, he believes that he could have played more robustly and assertively, but it was an effective strategy: Eva was able to sing with plenty of power and would captivate the audience with her beautiful voice.

The band members often quarrelled about expanding their repertoire. Eva had a preference for songs that lamented death and lost love. For Keith this was only part of the story. In his opinion, a musician had to try to capture an audience's attention and he didn't like the idea of force-feeding spectators with ballads that were difficult to understand. Overall, though, Eva and Keith largely had the same taste – they adored old R&B songs and ballads, and they shared a love for Ray Charles. They differed on their opinion of the man himself, though, Keith choosing to see him as a hero, while Eva was appalled that a musical genius could treat the women in his life with such little respect.

Among Eva's favourites was the traditional broadside ballad 'A Bold Young Farmer', also known, with slight variation in the lyrics, as 'The Butcher Boy', but the one song she hated to sing was Aretha Franklin's 'Respect'. Eva felt she could never live up to her heroine but if anyone came close to singing it as well as Aretha, it was Eva. Although she didn't like to include it on the set list, the guys would play it anyway and she would have to join in.

Eva's cousin Laura Bligh remembers how the band tried to generate publicity and excitement for their gigs. Guitarist Keith Grimes would call up the gig venue to ask who was performing that night, to which he'd say: "Oh, Eva Cassidy? That's fantastic! I've got to come! Can you give me directions how to get there?" Sadly, in most spots in town the approach failed to create much of a buzz. At Sully's in Chantilly, Virginia they performed to an audience of just five or six. Most of the time they played for free so they could at least promote themselves. The Eva Cassidy Band was certainly not a profitable business.

It's difficult to understand why they didn't break through. Everyone who witnessed Eva perform describes it as a life-changing event, but somehow the band wasn't able to reach a mass audience. Keith was especially frustrated by the fact that they were unable to make a living out of music. Each member of the band had to stick with their jobs, and they were exhausted whenever they played.

Al Dale did his best to convince Eva to use her youth and looks to win an audience over, but she wasn't interested in the glamour of showbusiness. He discovered just how difficult it was working with Eva when he arranged some publicity shots. She asked Al what she should wear and he knew exactly: a beautiful black dress. Eva had a dress that would do, so she put it on, added some make-up and entered the studio. When Al saw her, his throat became dry and he had difficulty breathing: she looked absolutely stunning. As soon as he was able, Al said: "Eva, you look really great." The photographer got to work and Al believed he had finally got through to Eva: he had created a blonde version of Linda Ronstadt.

Several days later they received the results of the shoot – glamorous photos that could be used on a future album cover or as promotional posters. Eva was asked to choose her favourite. She looked at the photographs, hesitated for a few seconds and concluded: "Nice pictures, but I don't think that's me." She didn't want to use her body to sell music and at her wishes only her face from the images was used. In spite of Al's attempts to dress Eva fashionably, she preferred her shorts, jeans, baggy T-shirts, clod-hopper shoes and hair tied back in a ponytail.

Eva's objection to changing her appearance was not the only obstacle to success. An even greater problem was her stage presence: she just stood there. She held her guitar or her microphone and looked at the floor for the greater part of the evening. She sometimes tried to tell jokes between songs, but this was usually unsuccessful. Most of the time she merely offered a polite "Thank you". To give the band a vocal stage presence, Keith was asked to introduce them and then each song, which was quite unusual for a guitarist and made some in the audience feel uneasy. When Keith talked, Eva would take a step back, coming forward only to sing again.

Al decided he had to do something. He began videotaping Eva and analysing the results with her. They practised dance moves to give Eva's performance a looser and lighter feel. Al showed her how to move from one side of the stage to the other, to give her performance a slightly entertaining twist. They rehearsed for days until she suddenly stopped, saying: "Al, this doesn't work for me. I'm not Madonna and I'm not Janet Jackson. I'm sorry to disappoint you." In the end all Al managed to do was to persuade Eva to click her fingers in time with the rhythm.

The worst engagement for The Eva Cassidy Band was at a country & western bar, Cotton Eyed Joe's in Temple Hills. Downstairs was reserved for a more successful band while Eva's group were upstairs. However, not one single visitor took the trouble of climbing the stairs, so they played without an audience. It was almost like a rehearsal.

At the other extreme, Eva's favourite gig was at Shootz pool hall. The entrance fee was $3, which meant $3 pool credit, and it had multiple TV screens, so the majority of punters weren't looking at her as she sang, which made it much easier for her to perform.

Between sets Eva would sometimes sit alone at a table. The other guys had to convince her to join them. She quickly became embarrassed, particularly if she received a compliment. But after several weeks things ran more smoothly. She had to adapt to being around a group of musicians in unfamiliar locations.

As the weeks went by and the gigs racked up Eva became more comfortable, showing her frustration only at things that went wrong onstage. She would never chide the other musicians, but if her guitar didn't have enough reverb or was out of tune, she could get angry, sometimes kicking the equipment in annoyance – a far cry from her first gig when she'd burst into tears as her microphone fell to the floor.

After a while Eva decided that her Gibson Chet Atkins guitar sounded too thin, so she and Chris went shopping for a new one. She finally found a great-sounding Yamaha, which was used on the recording of 'Over The Rainbow' that ended up on *The Other Side*. However, she soon discovered that the guitar was too large for her short arms to play properly. Chris bought the Yamaha off her and they returned to

Bethesda's music store where they found a Guild Songbird, the guitar she used for the rest of her life.

Eva couldn't tune a guitar herself, not even with an electric tuning device, so Keith Grimes or Mike Dove, her biggest fan since hearing the tapes Eva and Chris had made several years earlier, would help her out. Mike, who regularly came to the band's gigs, was happy to tune her guitar and discovered the reason for it dropping out of tune so often: Eva had strong hands – she was used to lifting heavy pots and plants at Behnke's, so she pulled the strings with the same force. The white Fender Stratocaster she sometimes used had a 'floating bridge' which led to tuning problems, but after a bit of practice Eva eventually got the hang of using an electric tuner.

One of the highlights of their live career was a gig in the summer of 1992 at a festival called Taste Of DC. They played after the much-acclaimed Little Feat in the middle of Pennsylvania Avenue on a stage in front of the Post Office. "We really kicked ass there," recalls Chris Biondo.

Since Eva was now performing regular gigs, Dan could see that his sister had made good progress. But a record contract still proved elusive, so he decided to help her. He knew a girl from Bowie who was in a relationship with Daniel Lanois, the world-famous producer of U2, Bob Dylan, Emmylou Harris and The Neville Brothers. Lanois lived in New Orleans, so Dan hopped on a plane with Chris and Eva's tapes stuffed in his luggage. But he never reached New Orleans: heavy snowstorms grounded the flight in Chicago. Dan still has the tapes in his possession today.

Eva's presence continued to be requested on diverse recordings. Local heroes Chuck Brown & The Soul Searchers recorded their seventh album, a collection of new songs, in the summer of 1991. Born in 1936, Chuck Brown grew up in a musical family and his mother encouraged him to sing from the age of two. He sang for people before he could even talk. From seven to 13 he played the piano in church. The family was very poor and Chuck's life was on the streets. As a youngster he was a shoeshine boy based at the Howard Theater, using the sales pitch: "Shine! Five cents, a nickel or half-a-dime." He shone the shoes of

Louis Armstrong and Louis Jordan; Hank Williams even gave the boy a 50 cent tip.

He was locked up several times between his 13th and 24th birthdays and was destined for a life of poverty, but jail gave him time to reflect on his life and he learned to play the guitar while incarcerated in Lorton Reformatory. "In the joint I got serious about music," Brown remembers. Fifteen years later he would return there with his band to perform.

In 1966 he started his first band, Chuck & The Soul Searchers, and invented go-go music. The band had a 1979 hit with a funky song called 'Bustin' Loose', which remained at the top of the soul charts for four weeks. It later became one of the most sampled songs in hip-hop. Today, he is recognised as "The Godfather of Go-Go" and is a legend in the capital city.

Chris Biondo was the sound engineer on Chuck's new album. At the end of a long recording session, Chris and Chuck would stay on to discuss the day's work. Chuck had found a bottle of vodka in Chris' office, a gift from a government employee who'd taken a trip to Russia, and he welcomed the idea of emptying it with its owner. While drinking expensive vodka out of plastic cups, Chuck Brown reflected on his situation. He was popular, but he wasn't well known outside of D.C. Chris empathised – he was facing the same struggles with his own band.

Chuck was also concerned about the changes he was seeing on the D.C. club circuit. The atmosphere had become increasingly violent, punters would enter with handguns and the use of cocaine and heroin was widespread. Chuck loved his music, and that he was still a successful artist definitely made things easier, but lately he had been thinking of changing his musical style. He longed to create a sophisticated, nuanced sound. He wondered whether the new album should be a jazz record. "Talking about jazz," Chris replied, "I recently recorded a singer you might like. She is also into jazz, although she is not pigeonholed that easily. Her name is Eva Cassidy." Chuck had never heard of her.

Chris put the tape in the deck and pressed play. Eva's version of the classic T-Bone Walker song 'Stormy Monday' came through the speakers. Chuck didn't say a word but nodded approvingly. They listened in silence as song after song played. Chuck was bowled over by Eva's majestic voice, her command of jazz and blues impressed him. "In what part of D.C. does she live?" Chuck asked. Chris told him she lived in Bowie. "What is a black girl like Eva doing in Bowie?" Chuck replied. It suddenly dawned on Chris that his friend really believed Eva's bluesy voice was that of a black girl. "She's not black Chuck," Chris laughed. "If this girl ain't black than I ain't black either!" Chuck responded, in total disbelief.

Chris liked the idea of producing a record with both Chuck and Eva. "I think that it is important that you two meet each other – I'll arrange a meeting as soon as possible," he promised. Chuck left modest Anita's Court and climbed into his white stretch limousine. He put on his sunglasses and pressed play on the tape. As he drove off, he whispered: "Chuck Brown and Eva Cassidy." It was light again. The future looked bright as well.

Chapter 7

Get In The Car!

Chuck Brown is one of the most popular artists in Washington, D.C. Several generations have grown up with his music and recently a street in the city was renamed Chuck Brown Way. Chuck loves being photographed by his fans because "there once was a time when the only people who wanted to take my picture was the police".

Brown's musical career proper began in the sixties when he played guitar with Jerry Butler & The Earls of Rhythm. In 1965 Brown joined Los Latinos where he discovered conga drums and the Latin beat. Looking to invent a new style of music, he created his own sound by combining jazz, blues, gospel, soul and African rhythms. He wrote transitions between the music so that it was played non-stop and added audience call and response, something he had picked up in church. Brown started a new band, calling it The Soul Searchers, and the new style of music became known as 'go-go' because it never really stopped.

As time went by many people began to associate go-go music with violent crowd behaviour. The *Washington Post* wrote about the burgeoning go-go scene: "As cocaine and violence began overwhelming D.C., some knuckleheads used go-go shows to settle petty arguments or develop reputations for themselves. Drug dealers set up open-air bazaars outside, and some bands often glorified these hustlers. By the mid-eighties, go-go – which could cram hundreds of sweaty, dancing youths into a venue and keep them grooving peacefully all night – was identified with the violence that occurred after the shows."

Chuck was incensed with the violence that had taken over the Washington go-go scene and he demanded that "young'uns" who fought during his show hug each other before he would continue. In the eighties he started to move away from go-go music, pushing jazz elements to the forefront of his music on the 1986 album *Go-Go Swing Live*, which featured songs by Duke Ellington, Johnny Mercer and James Moody.

When Chuck discovered that there had been a violent shooting on the D.C. club circuit in 1988, he decided to take action, recording an anti-violence anthem with several other go-go musicians. 'D.C. Don't Stand For Dodge City' was a modest hit single, but it was clear that the best days of go-go had passed. Chuck's 25-year marriage ended in 1989, and his son, Chuck Brown Junior, died in a car crash in 1990. Two years later Chuck & The Soul Searchers played at a club in Adams Morgan, a culturally diverse neighbourhood in the northwest of the city, where a 20-year-old man was shot not far from the stage. Something had to change.

Chuck's dream was to record a duet album with a female singer, such as those of his heroes Louis Armstrong (with Ella Fitzgerald) and Billy Eckstine (with Sarah Vaughan). In the summer of 1990, a week after first hearing Eva's tapes, Brown returned to Chris' studio. When he got out of his limousine he met a short, blonde, blue-eyed lady. She recognised the famed "Godfather of Go-Go" immediately. She knew he'd been impressed by her vocals. "Hi," she said, "I'm Eva." Chuck was taken by surprise, presuming the young lady to be a fan. She suddenly realised he had no clue who she was: "I'm Eva Cassidy. You know – Chris played my tape for you. You are Chuck Brown. I've heard so much about you." Chuck couldn't believe his ears. He grabbed her by the arm and rushed into Chris' basement – could it really be true that this young blonde girl, dressed innocently in shorts and T-shirt, was the same girl who had impressed him with such powerful vocals? Chris nodded his head in amusement. He was proud of the girl he had discovered.

Chuck and Eva shook hands, beginning a musical relationship that would do wonders for Eva's singing career. They began working at Chris' studio every week, initially recording the duet 'You've Changed'. Though they came from vastly different backgrounds, they seemed to gel. Chuck appreciated Eva's down-to-earth nature and he also appreciated her sly sense of humour. They shared a love of music in all its forms, the American Songbook in particular. Eva was thrilled that Chuck thought her interesting enough to work with.

Both musicians were perfectionists, but Chuck was not used to a fellow musician taking music so seriously. Go-go musicians just "did their thing" onstage and placed a great deal of emphasis on entertainment, which as ever was unimportant to Eva. This young lady would take him to a higher musical level.

They both enjoyed working in the studio. Eva had never been comfortable with a live audience and Chuck had become tired of performing. Chris was happy with the burgeoning musical relationship, since all his and manager Al Dale's attempts to win a record deal had failed, largely due to Eva's stubborn nature. In meetings with record companies she would keep quiet, piping up only to state her intentions: "Don't make me sing that pop crap." Eva was not someone who easily made concessions and with Chuck he could see her finally opening up to change.

Chris had decided it was time to stop trying to secure a solo record deal for Eva. The only possibility of making a record was to duet with Chuck. He secured the other members of The Eva Cassidy Band for sessions, but drummer JuJu House had changed musical tack and would not be available for every recording. It was time for an emergency call to a drum veteran.

Raice McLeod was born in New Zealand where he started his drumming career. He worked in Australia for some years and played for American troops in Vietnam. In 1972 he moved to England, together with the other members of his band, where they were based in London but played all over Europe. Raice performed with Petula Clark, The New Seekers and Cliff Richard and was on the road with Olivia Newton-John. Because of his success he decided to move to

America, travelling back to New Zealand only when his father became fatally ill.

Raice had been based in Washington, D.C. since the eighties, which is where he met Chris Biondo. Chris mentioned that he and Al were looking for a new drummer for The Eva Cassidy Band. "Would you like to join the band of the best female singer in the world?" Raice decided to audition. Hearing Eva's voice was a revelation. Several days into recording *The Other Side*, Raice received a panic-stricken call from Chris: "We're about to record a few songs with Chuck and Eva but Chuck's drummer JuJu hasn't appeared. No one knows where he is. Raice, can you help us out?" Raice didn't hesitate and jumped in his car immediately. The opportunity to play on a Chuck Brown record was very appealing.

That day the band recorded three songs and Chuck was delighted with the results. He stopped Raice before he left at the end of the session: "Can you do the rest of the album as well? Your style is exactly what I'm looking for."

The Other Side was released in 1992 through Liaison, Brown's own label. It was quite a success. Chuck and Eva were interviewed by Alona Wartofsky for the *Washington City Paper*. The piece appeared on November 20 and provided insight into the relationship between the two musicians:

If, as Chuck Brown says, his "go-go swing" records, which funked up Duke Ellington, Lionel Hampton, and James Moody, "opened the door" for young music fans unfamiliar with vintage jazz and pop standards, his new album, The Other Side, *closes that door behind them. "There are some people that will buy any new record that I put out just to find out what's on it, see how interesting it is. And I appreciate that," says Brown. For this one, he says, music shoppers will pick up the CD and look at the title. "Then they'll turn it round and look at the other side." He breaks up laughing as if he hasn't told that joke before.*

Brown's easy laugh punctuates his conversation and occasionally interrupts that of Cassidy, who seems to laugh very little. Their partnership is a study in contrasts. He's as dark and weathered as she is pale and raw. Posing for a photographer, Brown's a natural ham; Cassidy nervously twists her purse while waiting for her turn. He's as gregarious as she is diffident. Brown has been performing longer than his twenty-nine-year-old collaborator has been alive. And yet, as she rations out her Marlboro Lights to him, their partnership seems to be an ideal one.

You almost don't believe them, except that when Brown boasts about how talented Cassidy is, anyone who's heard The Other Side *knows he's right. And when Cassidy gushes that doing this album "has been the biggest thrill in my life," what would sound like a show-biz quote coming from anyone else is credible because she has already fidgeted her way through stories about singing four-part harmony with her family (her brother, Dan Cassidy, plays violin on* The Other Side's *'Fever') and performing in her junior-high-school chorus. She currently works a day job in Behnke's Nurseries not far from where she lives in Upper Marlboro; before she met Brown, she says, her career was comprised of "things where you meet record people but nothing really happens" and gigs with her own Eva Cassidy Band: "I wish that it had a different name," she says, "but that's what it ended up being."*

Brown doesn't consider The Other Side *a creative departure. "My roots is blues and jazz, and as everybody know, I created go-go music so that I could continue to eat. Because back in those days when I was doing blues and jazz, I couldn't eat. That's the bottom line. "Most of the songs that we're doing have always been done by one artist, either a man or a woman, but never with two people. Her voice and my voice had such chemistry," he says. "I listened to her range and I said, 'She sings this in the same key as Billie Holiday, and I can sing it an octave below that key.' I just knew it would work, and it worked.*

"To play go-go, you have to work so hard. You have to project so much energy in order to keep the crowd motivated. There's no such thing as relaxing go-go music. You can't relax and play go-go music; it's too energetic." Young go-go bands have that energy, he says, and some – Pleasure, Young Groovers, Backyard Band, Total Control – can "play music", not just beats. And now, it's their turn. "Hey, let the old man chill out for a while, slide to the side and do something a little more relaxing, and then come back and join the little go-go crew when the time is right.

Chris and Eva had begun a tentative romantic relationship in 1990, around the time Chris left his house in Anita's Court and found a new recording room in Glenn Dale. When Chris asked Eva to move in with him in a new house in Upper Marlboro (the house mentioned in the Chuck and Eva interview above) she asked her mother for advice. It was not until Barbara gave her approval that Eva had the nerve to take the plunge.

Chris and Eva lived like a perfectly normal couple. Eva found pleasure in the relatively large garden and she also helped Chris refurbish the house. She painted a faux marble design on their floor. Eva was very happy. She showed her love for Chris in a poem about miracles that she wrote for him about the simple pleasures of life that "we can watch together, you standing next to me".

Chris was patient and attentive and he encouraged Eva during her moments of uncertainty. She was not always easy to understand, but Chris really did his best. He was Eva's biggest fan and he found delight in her music and art. They enjoyed swimming, cycling, walking with his dog, Bernice, and renting movies. Eva wasn't a great cook and most of the time they ate pizzas, hot dogs and tuna sandwiches. She wore his jeans, shirts and a pair of work boots.

They holidayed together, the Virgin Islands a favourite destination. They enjoyed swimming, paddling and snorkelling in the azure sea. Eva even summoned up the courage to sing at open-mic nights in a club called Barnacle Bill, her performance a sharp contrast to the other tourists' karaoke fare. During a visit to Florida, Chris stepped on a stingray on the beach and had an allergic reaction, dropping to the ground and fainting. Eva helped him to walk to an emergency doctor. She saved Chris' life.

In the early nineties several of Eva's friends and family got married, and she was invited to perform at their weddings. Two aspects of these performances were remarkable: Eva wore beautiful dresses and her choice of songs became notorious. At the wedding of her half sister, Anette, she played the Hank Williams standard 'Your Cheating Heart', and for her good friends Ruth and Jim she thought it appropriate to sing Simon & Garfunkel's 'Bridge Over Troubled Water'. She performed

Claire Hamill's 'You Take My Breath Away' during the wedding service of Celia Murphy and her husband, the lyrics of which appeared on the surface to be romantic. Most of the congregation were probably unaware that the song was about God, not a romantic relationship. Eva, herself, would never become a bride.

Since the album they made together sold fairly well, Chris decided to book Chuck and The Eva Cassidy Band for two performances at the Blues Alley in Georgetown, Washington, D.C. Eva was scared, but she knew she had to face up to her fears.

Al Dale convinced Eva to wear a dress onstage. Strangely enough she didn't find it difficult wearing feminine clothing in the presence of Chuck Brown. It was as if his masculinity stimulated her femininity. He certainly caught the attention of the mainly black audience with his striking presence, his cowboy hat, ponytail and sunglasses, which put Eva at ease. Although Al beseeched her to relax, snap her fingers and move a bit, Chuck stole the show. He was used to entertaining large groups of people and Blues Alley was a piece of cake for him. He danced, joked, sang and played as if the jazz joint was his second home.

Those in the audience got the impression that Chuck and Eva were a couple. Their love duets sounded more than convincing, but in reality it was simply a close friendship; Chuck lost his bravura in her company and she was less shy in his. They brought out the best in each other. Eva began to feel comfortable with or without a guitar and she was able to concentrate fully on her singing. Chuck dared to take risks with the new band, experimenting with the jazz sound, and his guitar playing improved every day. The rest of the band felt a bit intimidated by the large horn section, but the whole effect was fantastic.

Live they played more or less the same songs from the album – 'Fever', 'You Don't Know Me', 'You've Changed', 'Dark End Of The Street' and 'Drown In My Own Tears'. Eva altered some songs so that they sounded more jazz-like. The owner of the Blues Alley, Ralph Camilli, was impressed by her abilities and promised Chris that they could come back some day.

Stage fright never left Eva completely but her performances with Chuck saw her worst fears subside. Together with Chuck, The Eva

Cassidy Band attracted bigger audiences all over town. In the beginning, they returned for the "Godfather of Go-Go", but soon word got round about the blonde singer in his band.

They played at the Columbia Arts Festival in 1993, and opened for singing soul preacher Al Green at the Stone Soul Picnic, which drew 20,000 visitors to Northeast Washington. At Wolf Trap they opened for the famous Neville Brothers. The audience was surprised by Chuck's new sound and the crowd really responded to Eva. They also performed successfully in the Grand Foyer at the Kennedy Center.

Al Dale continued to send material to record labels. Bruce Lundvall, head of the famous jazz label Blue Note, showed some interest. Al and Eva decided to travel by train to New York to meet with Lundvall and, in his office, she sang several songs with guitar accompaniment including 'Autumn Leaves' and a stunning a cappella version of 'Amazing Grace'. The record exec was clearly impressed by the young female singer and advised them to get a decent demo together to show what an Eva Cassidy album would embody. He even gave them a small budget since he really believed in the project.

Eva wasn't too keen on New York so instead of lingering in the big city they returned to Washington, D.C. immediately by the fast Amtrak train from Penn Station.

The next day they recorded the tape that would help Eva take the biggest step in her career. She chose her four favourite songs, all very different: 'Wayfaring Stranger', 'Oh, Had I A Golden Thread', 'Blues In The Night' and 'Nightbird'. 'Wayfaring Stranger' was recorded with JuJu House on drums. Eva decided on the sound and atmosphere of the track, suggesting Keith quote a lick from 'I'm Coming Home Baby', the original of which was sung by Mel Tormé and composed by Ben Tucker and Bob Dorough, and he played this in ascending octaves, giving the recording its characteristic strength. Eva invented a bass line for Chris and asked Kent Wood to play his Fender Rhodes in the style of Ray Charles and JuJu to use his brushes.

They recorded several takes and sent the best versions to Bruce Lundvall. After listening to the tape he still believed that Eva had what it took to become a success, but first she had to decide on a direction.

Stylistically, her music was too diverse. Eva responded by saying that she liked to sing songs she loved and that all she knew was the difference between a good and a bad song. "I don't want to be pigeon-holed," she said. "I just want to sing, and I certainly don't want to restrict myself to jazz." Lundvall admired Eva's determination, but he couldn't make a record under these conditions.

Apollo Records, a subsidiary branch of Motown Records in New York, had also grown interested in Eva, to the point that its representatives travelled down to the studio in D.C. to hear her for themselves. Unusually, they were also intrigued by Eva's art, since an Apollo employee also organised art exhibitions in the Big Apple. Eva brought some of her paintings to Chris' studio and everything looked promising. Apollo gave Chris, Al and Eva a cheque for a demo, and Eva took to recording again.

Once the tape was done, Chris and Eva travelled back to New York to the luxurious Apollo offices on the top floor of the famous Apollo Theatre on 125th Street in Harlem. Apollo was keen and promised to show up with a contract. Soon after, the record company was pronounced bankrupt.

MCA Records (now part of Universal Music Group) had also shown an interest. It sent its A&R guys to check Eva out, but she perceived them to be arrogant, something she couldn't stand. She was just too obstinate to fit into MCA's corporate structure.

During this period of back and forth with various interested parties, Eva was going through a serious gospel phase. She enjoyed going to Carter Barron Amphitheatre in Washington D.C. to see BeBe & CeCe Winans. Chris joined her and although he liked the uplifting character of the music, he was sceptical of the compulsively happy preachers. Eva would later record several gospel tracks, directly influenced by this period in her life.

Al Dale and Blue Note's Bruce Lundvall continued to talk. Bruce had decided that Eva's tape was too varied. "I just don't know what to do with you," he would say. However he didn't want to lose Eva, so he offered her a guest vocalist slot on another artist's album.

Pieces Of A Dream was a modern, successful jazz group, which suited Eva well. She and Al travelled to a recording studio in Philadelphia where Eva would record two songs for the group's new album, *Goodbye Manhattan*, released in 1994. But even this wasn't without problems: the producer recorded Eva line by line, which made her feel like she was in a straitjacket. She didn't get the chance to show what she was capable of. "This is how I work," the producer remarked, after several pleas from Al and Eva to change his method.

Despite the disagreements in the studio, Eva joined the group on a short tour to promote their album. They performed in several clubs in Philadelphia and New York and even on a jazz cruise, an evening of fine dining and jazz on a large boat.

In November 1993 Eva and Chris received an invitation to The Wammies, the Washington Area Music Association Awards, an annual award ceremony held at the Hilton Hotel in Washington. Eva had a pottery class that same evening so she declined the invitation. Several days later Chris got a phone call from Mike Schreibman, president of the WAMA. He strongly advised Chris to attend the ceremony with Eva (although he couldn't say exactly why).

The reason for this soon became clear. That evening Eva won her first Wammie for Best Female Vocalist. When she came forward to accept the prize, Al and Chris stood up and cheered, but the rest of the audience didn't have the faintest idea who she was. Eva, too, was baffled. She hesitated for a moment, before saying, "Thank God. And I'd like to thank my mom and dad, my manager Al Dale, Chris Biondo and Chuck Brown. Thank you very much." After the ceremony a local reporter asked her to comment on her success. "This is exciting," she said. "I feel like I'm allowed into the club of Washington musicians now."

While the Pieces Of A Dream album was a great opportunity for Eva, solo success still proved elusive. The other members of The Eva Cassidy Band were left bitterly disappointed with developments. Keith Grimes compares Blue Note's refusal to contract Eva to that of Decca passing on The Beatles. "It was not necessary to ask Eva to stick to a jazz repertoire. A few years later they changed their minds and contracted another female singer with a wide-ranging repertoire. Norah Jones would become the biggest-selling Blue Note artist ever. What's more,

Norah Jones saved Blue Note. Eva was in the same position as Norah Jones and Bruce Lundvall regrets his decision. He admitted that in TV interviews, which was very humble of him." However bitter he was at the time, Keith now forgives Lundvall, conceding that, "He was serious about music. For him, like for Eva, it was a matter of selling quality music and not only a matter of making profits."

The only thing left was to return to shows for live audiences, and when they did they discovered that thanks to the recent recording work Eva's singing had continued to improve. They shared the opinion that their playing was essentially subservient to her voice: you'll rarely hear an Eva fan comment on Keith's marvellous guitar solos or Raice's drum lick. There were no egos in this band. Chris, Lenny, Keith and Raice allowed her to flourish and Eva felt safe with the guys around her. The boys wanted her to sound good and feel at ease. If Raice saw her shrinking on stage, he knew he was playing too loudly and would tone it down.

Chris Biondo says of the band: "There are four guys in a car. Suddenly they see a lonely girl walking along the road. The guys called to her: 'Get in the car and we'll take you to wherever you need to go.'" The Eva Cassidy Band was a means of transport for Eva to reach her destiny. Without the band she would have remained a hitchhiker all her life.

Still, she continued to feel an element of uncertainty. She knew she could sing, but she always requested reverb. But she communicated the message of the songs so well that listeners reacted in a deeply emotional manner to her. She didn't need gimmicks or special lighting: Eva could transform a room with her voice.

Technically she might have had her limits on the guitar but she wrote her own guitar parts and she knew exactly what she wanted. She was also a powerful arranger: she removed everything that overpowered the song, retaining the essential core. It was a gift that would see such classics as 'Over The Rainbow' and 'American Tune' come to be known as her own.

The second time Eva was invited to the Wammies ceremony, in 1994, she was asked to sing. WAMA president Mike Schreibman gave her the choice to perform with or without the band. She decided that she would perform solo versions of 'Time After Time' and 'Over The Rainbow' which she had now perfected and wanted to unveil to the world. Mike was concerned: "It's a big hall and the crowd will be noisy – are you sure?"

Sure enough, as Eva finished 'Time After Time' and started to sing 'Over The Rainbow' there was a murmur of laughter. One audience member was heard to say, "Don't tell me that this girl is trying to do this sentimental song from *The Wizard Of Oz* in this place?" But Eva persevered and sang convincingly with enormous presence. The room settled down, absorbed, and when the last notes faded away there was complete silence for a few seconds before the audience erupted in prolonged applause.

Grace Griffith and Marcy Marxer, two popular singers from the D.C. area that Eva adored, found Eva during the interval – they wanted to express their admiration. It wasn't a unique situation for Eva to face, but her shyness often held her back in such company. She would have to get over her nervousness quickly.

In 1994 Mick Fleetwood, founder and drummer of Fleetwood Mac, opened a nightclub in an inconspicuous office building in Alexandria, Virginia, calling it Fleetwood's. Many local bands performed there and Mick would sometimes join in for a couple of impromptu numbers. Mick was bowled over with The Eva Cassidy Band: the mix of American folk rock with a clear European twist was right up his street. He joined them onstage, and in this way Eva got to perform with a much-admired hero.

Mick was surprised to discover that the band was unsigned. He promised to help them and offered his services for future recordings. He advised Eva to narrow her focus: she simply had to choose between jazz, blues or folk. But, true to form, Eva responded: "If the record company won't let me sing songs that mean something to me, I don't want to work with them."

Chapter 8

I Don't Want To Be Any Man's Bride

Since 1981, Eva had worked at Behnke's Nurseries, a multi-acre facility in Largo. Initially she worked for the growing department as a transplanter. She would work in the greenhouse, watering, transplanting seedlings, pinching and tying poinsettias. Her older sister, Anette, also worked there part time while she completed her nursing degree.

In the nineties Eva left the growing department and became the only female crew member to work in Behnke's woody plants department, which gave her the opportunity to be outside. Perennial specialist Larry Hurley remembers Eva very well: "In those days our peat moss came in six-cubic-foot bales, loose on a semi. They were unloaded by hand and stacked in a warehouse. We looked like a bunch of ants. Including Ant One – me – muttering to myself and dragging a bale, and Ant Two – Eva – with a bale of peat as big as she, balanced on her shoulder, climbing up a mountain of bales. She was only 5' 2", but loaded many trees right alongside the guys."

Being the only woman on·a crew of nurserymen toughened Eva up. Most of the time she was dressed in an olive-coloured uniform and the work she had to do was hard and dirty, including potting, watering, weeding, moving heavy plants around and driving a forklift truck. Her supervisor, Dave Nizinski, gave her some additional duties including woody plant propagation. Many people in Maryland still have plants in their gardens that were produced by Eva. The cycle of life goes on.

In 1993, Eva continued to struggle with self-esteem and was concerned about a small mole on her nose, which she thought looked awful. She went to see a dermatologist who removed it but on closer examination the dermatologist discovered a larger spot on Eva's back. Concerned, she advised Eva to have a biopsy, so Chris and Eva went to Prince George's County Hospital where Eva underwent a further, lengthier examination. Chris spent many hours in the waiting room until Eva and the doctor finally returned. The doctor then showed them several scans that indicated the patch on Eva's back was malignant melanoma. The doctor subsequently removed a large strip of skin from Eva's back, and assured her that the cancerous cells had all been removed, but he also urged her to keep an eye on her health and check in regularly with her doctor. A few weeks later Eva followed up with an appointment with an oncologist to see if the cancer had spread, which wasn't the case then. Eva made no further such appointments.

When Eva returned to work she tried to stay covered up while working in the sun, requesting more indoor work. But she hated being in an office and particularly despised computers. The phrase, "Did you remember to log in?" became a recurring joke between her and colleagues.

Eva's mother remained important in her life and they still spent Sunday afternoons together, walking, hiking and biking in southern Maryland's countryside. Barbara was completely in tune with her complicated daughter. They were able to talk as friends.

In 1994 Barbara and Eva took a trip to Europe where they visited Barbara's hometown, Bad Kreuznach. Eva loved German architecture, the farmhouses, the thatched roofs and the European cows. In the final week of May 1994, along with Barbara's sister, Katrin, they travelled further south to Greece. They hiked together across the Greek island Samos and Eva concluded that the Nightingale Valley was "heaven".

It was at a hotel in Nightingale Valley that Eva gave her first European performance. She had bought a small guitar and she performed on the roof, under the starry sky. Days later she was told that everyone in the neighbourhood had opened their windows to hear this angelic voice. In fact, she was such a hit with the locals that they didn't want her to leave – when would they ever get to hear her beautiful voice again?

Eva also enjoyed spending time with her cycling friend, Elaine Stonebreaker, the sister of Lynn Stonebreaker, whom Eva met at Bowie High, and who would later take the famous photograph that was used on the cover of Eva's 1998 album *Songbird*. The girls would undertake an annual cycling trip down the towpath along the Chesapeake & Ohio Canal, an impressive route of 185 miles from Georgetown, not far from Blues Alley, to Harper's Ferry.

Elaine adored the music of Grace Griffith, a Celtic folk singer, as did Eva. Together they went to see her perform in Farthing's Ordinary Tavern in St. Mary's City, Maryland's colonial capital. Eva admired Grace's musical style and her controlled way of singing and she would attend her concerts whenever she got the chance. The respect was mutual. Grace had heard about this singer "who could really wail" and she quickly placed the familiar face when she witnessed Eva's performance at the Wammies.

Eva was still friends with her former boyfriend Ned Judy who had returned to Maryland from California. They, too, enjoyed cycling along the St. Mary's River State Park Trails in south Maryland. She also spent many evenings with her school friend Ruth Murphy and her fiancé Jim Dickey. They worked together on all kinds of craft projects, including making pottery and baking cakes with beautifully decorated marzipan layers. They spent hours making comical home movies in which they dressed in costume, taking to their roles with aplomb in their *Gorillas In The Mist* parody 'Chickens In The Mist'.

Eva's relationship with Ruth's elder sister Celia continued to improve: she was someone who really understood Eva, to the point where they sometimes shared an innate telepathy. On one occasion Celia was working in Crystal City when she received a phone message: "Celia, I'm in Alexandria and I am at the store that I know you really like. If you want to see me, come to Alexandria. I have my bike." Why hadn't Eva told her what store? Alexandria was huge – how would she find her? But she decided to set off anyway, driving to the Zipia fashion store. When she arrived, there was Eva, standing outside the store with her bike. When she saw Celia her mouth fell open: "How did you find me?"

It was not particularly "cool" for young people to talk about religious matters, but Eva and Celia's spirituality brought them closer together. Eva asked Celia to write down the lyrics to 'Morning Has Broken', Cat Stevens' arrangement of the 1931 hymn by Eleanor Farjeon. "You'd better have the words right," Eva said, "because God is listening too." The girls took their religion seriously, but they didn't let it spoil their sense of humour. Driving along one sunny afternoon and belting out a beautiful hymn, a noisy lorry overtook them, ruining the song. They didn't miss a beat: "Asshole!"

Eva was also very fond of her cousin Walter Wunderlich, a cabinetmaker like many of Barbara's relatives, who lived in Nova Scotia, Canada. She and Barbara regularly visited Walter and his mother, Barbara's cousin Dorothee, in the maritime province. In fact, the photograph on the cover of Eva's 2002 album *Imagine* was taken by Walter in Nova Scotia. Eva painted two impressive canvasses here: *Cape John*, named after the place where she watched the moon rise and witnessed several meteor showers; and *Nova Scotia Cow*, created to reflect the peace and quiet she found on the Canadian island.

Eva's friendships were all-important to her, particularly as she was beginning to see her relationship with Chris in a different light. She had hoped the connection with Biondo would grow and become more spiritual, but instead she felt trapped. However, she hated to hurt anyone's feelings, and Chris remained very important to her: he was her mentor, her bass player and her producer and he stimulated her creativity. Yet something wasn't right, and she summed up her feelings to her mother: "As soon as men start an intimate relationship, they think they own you." She saw her situation in the lyrics of one of her favourite songs, 'Tall Trees In Georgia', which compares the shade beneath tall trees to the breakdown of a relationship and includes the line: "The sweetest love I ever had I left aside/Because I did not want to be any man's bride."

Eva asked for a temporary time out. It was high time to decide what she wanted to do with her life.

During his year spent living and travelling all over Germany, Dan Cassidy had discovered that Europeans appreciated his way of playing. He felt very much at ease on the continent and close to his roots. When he arrived in Iceland he felt completely at home and decided to make it his home. He still resides there today.

Iceland is a military, geographic and cultural bridge between Europe and America. Dan loved the clean air, the bright water, the down to earth nature of the people and their love for art, literature and music. He soon became an in-demand fiddler because of his ability to turn his hand to jazz, blues and folk. He invited his sister to visit him in 1994.

Eva arrived with her mother and also fellow Stonehenge band member Larry Melton, with whom she kept up a close friendship. Dan had played Eva's tapes to the owner of the Blues Bar in Reykjavik, Jonas Helgason, and he agreed to her performing five nights a week over her three-week stay.

When Eva played for an Icelandic audience they listened in absolute silence. Dan was able to see that she was still improving and that there had been a significant change in her musical choices, from jazz and blues towards real folk ballads. She even performed the classic rhythm and blues song 'Ain't No Sunshine' as a folk ballad.

Eva was a great success in Iceland. The audiences were respectful of her music and they showed their appreciation, sitting in a quiet circle around the stage. She even began to socialise with her audiences after shows. Icelandic people love to drink and Eva had her fair share. It was as if she had been freed from her inner chains.

Eva went down so well in her first-week performances that the following week she found herself on the front page of the culture supplement of Icelandic newspaper *Pressan* and she was invited to play live on the radio. She performed one of her favourite ballads, Simon & Garfunkel's 'Bridge Over Troubled Water'.

It was on the trip to Iceland that Eva was introduced to Anna Karen Kristinsdóttir who was born there in 1965. Anna Karen became a member of several Icelandic bands, through whom she met Eva's brother. Dan felt at ease in her presence because of her uplifting, outgoing and light nature: she likes to meet new people and she empathises with those around her, although she has to admit she sometimes trusts people too easily. Like Eva, Anna Karen enjoyed singing a wide range of music, from jazz and blues to pop and rock. She would become a very important and much-loved friend to Eva.

Eva met Anna Karen after one of her performances at the Blues Bar. Anna Karen saw a beautiful and smiling, but shy girl. Dan felt they would connect, despite their different approaches to performing: Anna Karen's outgoing nature led her to sing and dance and talk extensively to the audience between songs. Still, she was in awe of the girl from Maryland. "I wish I possessed a tenth of the musical talents of Eva," she said, and told Eva as much.

She invited Eva to her home and they talked for hours. Anna Karen saw that the Cassidy siblings had much in common but she recognised one important difference: Dan knew exactly what he wanted, his boundaries were very clear and he was disciplined. Eva was introverted, but she had the desire to break out of her hermit's cell. Her seclusion was not voluntary; she had a craving for living life to the full and Anna Karen resolved to help her do just that.

Eva felt safe in Anna Karen's presence and she told her things she'd never dreamed of telling anyone before. Anna Karen recognised a kindred soul, bursting with zest for life and, little by little, she did her best to help Eva overcome this fear of life and other people. She hugged her, saying, "Don't be afraid, there is nothing to worry about. You are okay; there is nothing wrong with you." She made Eva hot baths, gave her perfume and mixed nice cocktails for her. Eva's fears didn't dissipate immediately, but Anna Karen's treatment certainly began to take effect. The quiet girl from Maryland gradually learned to love herself, to accept her body and to enjoy life. Eva flew back to America knowing she had found a true friend and soulmate.

Something else had happened in Iceland. Eva had realised she needed to make some radical decisions, the most important of which affected her relationship with Chris Biondo. She didn't want to lose his friendship, but she needed space. And she wanted to change her musical direction, not only from jazz and blues to folk, but she had also grown tired of having to discuss every song choice with the other band members. She finally accepted what she had known and been scared of for a long time: she wanted to strike out on her own.

Jackie Fletcher came from West Virginia and bought a large house in Annapolis. She met Larry Melton at Smith's guitar factory where she worked as a financial administrator and they soon became friends. She met "the Bowie kids", as she called them, including Eva, at one of their gatherings in 1993. The Bowie friends were younger than her, but Jackie liked them and she shared their passion for music. She saw that Eva was much-loved and that this special girl needed extra care.

During one of their conversations Jackie discovered that Eva was reluctant to confront Chris about her feelings. She was too nervous to leave him. But while Chris was not at home, Jackie, Hugh and Larry helped her to move out. They packed all her things and took them to her parents' home in Bowie. Chris was not happy, but Eva's leaving didn't come completely out of the blue for him.

It was a difficult decision to make: while Eva was gone Margret had moved into her old room, an apartment that Hugh had built for her, with its own entrance and a small kitchen. Eva had to take the only empty room, a small downstairs bedroom that she used for a couple of nights.

Eva loved her parents, but she had grown distant from them, confiding to Dan that she felt she didn't really know her mother any more. While Barbara was a good listener, she was the product of a conventional forties upbringing and very rarely shared her true feelings. In a letter to Dan in Iceland Eva wrote about her relationship with her father, mentioning that Hugh had let down his 'stone wall' during a bike ride they took together on the C&O Canal around the time Hugh had hurt his back and needed her help. They had enjoyed each other's company for a change and hung out together while Barbara was visiting Germany. Usually, though, Eva found it difficult to see beyond Hugh's detached exterior and gauge his true feelings.

Jackie Fletcher decided to offer Eva a room in her big house in Annapolis. Eva visited first and they took a cycling tour of the neighbourhood, since it was not only important to see something of the surroundings but also to assess whether they would enjoy each other's company. They visited a gallery and they bought an ice cream. Eva decided to stay the night. When she looked out of the window from the bed and saw how beautiful the moon looked silhouetted against the sky, she made up her mind: "I'll take it."

The view was indeed affecting. It was a very old house, in fact some locals believed it to be haunted. An early owner had kept slaves in the grounds and rumour had it that the slaves had returned after their death, a story that made a huge impression on Eva. She enjoyed ghost stories, and she was as fascinated by the history of slavery as she was appalled by its cruelty.

Eva surrounded herself with fresh flowers, vintage hats and old pieces of furniture she bought at second-hand stores that she painted in light pastels. She filled the house with her arts and crafts. She was prolific, creating new things every day from clay, glass, copper, tin, oil, beads and trinkets. Although Eva appreciated her newfound freedom and loved the house, Jackie was a bit older than her and could be very outspoken. Eva, in contrast, always needed time to think before she voiced her opinions. She talked deliberately, as if every word was important to her. She began to feel cautious in Jackie's presence. When Eva arrived home after a long day's work she would go up to her room, preferring her own company as she always had.

Anna Karen visited them regularly from Iceland, Jackie even making up a guest room especially for Eva's best friend. On one such visit she organised a party for Eva's 32nd birthday. Eva enjoyed her birthday cake but suddenly left the other guests, retreating into her room. No one took it personally – Eva's friends knew that time alone was precious to her. She never did anything because others wanted her to and she never followed the crowd. Eva was always busy in her head: she had no room for social niceties.

Jackie asked Eva to help with cleaning and odd jobs around the house but Eva resisted, preferring to pay Jackie to do it because, as she put it, "I don't do chores." She was extremely focused on her music and art and she couldn't afford to be disturbed during the creative process. But Jackie insisted that Eva be responsible for her "own apartment", meaning she was left to clean her own kitchen block. There were two exceptions to the rule: they shared the responsibility for the bathroom and in wintertime they worked outside together to clear snow, which was often very deep.

Despite their personality differences, Eva and Jackie would have interesting conversations about life, music, art and friendship. They discussed civil rights, discrimination and the horror of slavery. Many people still had distorted views about this dark chapter in history, including Jackie whose parents had told her that "slavery hadn't been that bad at all". Such white propaganda had been influential during the Civil Rights Movement in the sixties and many white people in Maryland still held prejudiced views.

Eva's views were quite the opposite. She admired black culture, especially black music, and she liked to socialise with black people. She was not a great reader but she was passionate about Etta James' autobiography and Alice Walker's novel *The Color Purple*.

Written in 1982 and set in Georgia in the thirties, *The Color Purple* is built around several themes that fascinated Eva. The main character, Celie, has been oppressed by men her whole life and is introverted because of it. Slavery was still a recent memory in Georgia at the time the story takes place, yet men continue to dominate women and Celie finds it hard to deal with. Shug Avery is Celie's opposite, brave and outspoken. She helps Celie to develop emotionally and spiritually, giving her hope and inspiration. She influences not only the way in which Celie allows her husband, Albert, to treat her, but her religious views as well. Initially Celie sees God as a white man, but Shug tells her that God has no race or gender.

Celie discovers that female relationships can be sisterly and safe. She and Shug come across a field of purple flowers and Shug tells her to embrace their beauty despite her unhappy life: "You must look at all the good and acknowledge them because God planted them on earth."

Celie is able to show real emotions only in her letters. The letters symbolise the inner voice of Celie in the same way that Eva chose to perform certain songs because of their lyrical importance to her. After Celie's divorce she starts to work as a trouser maker. The trousers symbolise the feminist theme that runs throughout the book in a way that Eva very much took to heart.

In 1985, the novel was adapted into a film directed by Steven Spielberg and starring Whoopi Goldberg and Oprah Winfrey. Eva loved it and watched it dozens of times. Some critics found the portrayal of black men as abusive and disloyal off-putting. Others chided Spielberg for cutting the lesbianism in the novel out of his film. Still, the film became a huge success, grossing over $142 million worldwide and being nominated for 11 Academy Awards (none of which it won). The film's power lies not only in its themes and excellent acting, but in its music, a potent mix of gospel and blues, which of course lifted Eva's spirit.

Jackie and Eva had long discussions about religion and spirituality. As a child Eva had found relief in Christianity, but after several years had stopped attending church regularly. In the beginning of her relationship with Chris Biondo she went through a gospel phase, which saw them attend many gospel concerts together and she was actively involved in gospel music. Songs such as 'Wayfaring Stranger (I'm Going There To See My Saviour)', 'People Get Ready', 'Wade In The Water' and 'How Can I Keep From Singing?' were hugely meaningful to Eva. But Eva was not and never would be an Evangelical Christian. In John Lennon's 'Imagine' she sings convincingly: "Imagine there's no heaven, it's easy if you try/ No hell below us, above us only sky."

Hugh Cassidy was brought up in the All Souls Unitarian Church, a branch of the Unitarian Universalism religion. His mother, Clara Cassidy, had been a member of this church in the fifties and sixties. According to Eva's cousin Laura Bligh, who is also a member of this church, UU members are usually "secular-humanist-intellectual-liberals". A facet of the religion is for its members to continue to grow spiritually.

Unitarianism and Universalism are rooted in Christian faith. In the United States the Unitarian movement began in the congregational parish churches of New England, which were part of the state church of Massachusetts. New England Unitarians rejected the emphasis on the chosen few that the Puritan Pilgrim Fathers had preached. Instead, they believed that "all were universally saved", i.e. that all persons and creatures are related to a God or the Divine and will be reconciled to God. UU members prefer to speak about the spirit of life rather than about deities. Their theology is based upon search and not authority. They believe in the dignity of every person and in justice, equity and compassion in human relations. Their ultimate goal is peace, liberty and justice for all.

UU Sunday services resemble the form of Protestant worship in the Reformed tradition. Such a service includes hymn-singing, accompanied by organ, piano, or other instruments, sometimes led by a song leader or choir. Their hymns vary from traditional tunes with new lyrics, spirituals, folk songs from various cultures, to original compositions by UU musicians. Members of this religion have often been active in political causes, and in 1984 the UU was the first major church to approve religious blessings on homosexual unions.

Hugh Cassidy was brought up as a Unitarian Universalist and in later life went through several spiritual phases. His religious views are a curious mix of the serious and the strange, from Christianity to outer space and UFOs, but at the end of Eva's life he was heavily influenced by the works of Edgar Cayce (1877–1945). His bookshelves are crammed with biographies and studies about the so-called "sleeping prophet" and he urged Eva to read them. Hugh was a member of a group that met to discuss meditation, reincarnation and spiritualism.

Unlike his brothers John and Lew, who were intellectuals like their father, Hugh didn't go to college. As such, his power lifting was some sort of compensation, helping to temper his inferiority complex. Edgar Cayce's own education stopped at the ninth grade and this resonated with Hugh. Cayce proved that it was not necessary to be a professor to have original opinions about big questions of the universe. That Cayce called himself a Christian made it easier to accept his deviating spiritual theories. Cayce had been a member of The Disciples of Christ his entire life and he read the Bible every day. After he was struck by laryngitis, Cayce lost his speech completely in 1900. His voice returned after he was treated by "Hart the Laugh Man", a travelling hypnotist and entertainer who put Cayce into a trance to cure his lost voice. While in the hypnotic state Cayce said things that he had no way of knowing consciously. To those who saw this, they believed he possessed special powers.

As soon as the news spread, several people with illnesses came to visit him. It wasn't always necessary to be present during a healing session, however – a letter including a person's name and location was often enough to gain a diagnosis and remedy. The commercially minded tried to use Cayce's supposed powers to gain fame and fortune, but Cayce was against making money from his patients.

Cayce started to believe that his information came from spirits who had lived and died on earth. During a great part of his life he investigated this area and he wrote many books about the twilight zone between the Christian notion of a unique individual that was responsible for his own life and the idea that everyone received more opportunities than just one lifetime to become a good person. Little by little Cayce saw dying as entering again into the presence of the Creator, as he states: "All souls were created in the beginning, and they are finding their way back to whence we came."

Cayce was able to find a bridge between Buddhism and what we nowadays would call New Age thinking by saying: "As ye sow, so shall ye reap" and "As ye judge others, so shall ye be judged." He was also one of the first spiritualists to see the benefits of meditation, which became popular decades after his death. Meditation, Cayce believed, was a way of opening up to divine influences. Through prayer we speak to God, but in meditation He speaks to us. Cayce also believed that God could speak to us in dreams.

Eva Cassidy shared her father's interest in Cayce, although she wasn't as fascinated by the dogma. Although uninvolved in any form of organised religion, she was a spiritual person who also believed in the afterlife, reincarnation and angels. When she stayed at Johns Hopkins Hospital Eva read *A Book Of Angels* by Sophie Burnham, an author who lives in Maryland. Burnham reflects on angels past and present and explains how they touch people's lives. In truth, it is difficult to be specific about what Eva actually believed in. Her friend Celia Murphy noticed that Eva was attracted by the 'Good Samaritan' aspect of the Bible, and Keith Grimes remembers the relief Eva showed when he told her of his own belief in reincarnation.

Jackie was also helpful in Eva's day-to-day life. Eva barely ever cooked meals and she liked to eat fatty foods, tuna sandwiches being about the only healthy thing she ate. Jackie tried to convince her of the importance of organic food, but it was difficult; Eva had learned bad habits from gigging around town, where after a performance she would stop along the road at a fast-food restaurant or a gas station to buy junk food. Sometimes Jackie would resort to cooking vegetables from her own garden and taking them upstairs to Eva in her room.

Jackie also helped Eva with her finances. Although she was never late with rent, Eva didn't have a proper bank account and she showed no interest in money: "I didn't notice that petrol prices have risen... I still get $20 worth," she once told Jackie.

The two would spend time discussing Eva's relationship with Chris, Jackie discovering that there were two sides to the story. Chris was not afraid to be blunt and he was difficult in an argument. He didn't listen to Eva, but she admitted that she'd found it hard to make her feelings clear. "Eva didn't need the baggage of someone else," Biondo said about Eva's leaving him. Despite their differences, the two remained close friends and they even went on holiday together after the split. She had felt hemmed in by the relationship, but they remained loyal friends.

Jackie taught Eva to be more assertive, making it possible to discuss all kinds of little issues that had grown into mountainous problems in Eva's mind. Many of these were related to The Eva Cassidy Band. She believed she had lost control musically, that the other band members ignored her ideas. Jackie tried to instil in Eva that without her there would be no Eva Cassidy Band: she was the band's leader and its namesake – and also its greatest asset.

Eva's new home town of Annapolis was the perfect place for small or solo gigs. The old town had plenty of bars and restaurants interested in low-profile and acoustic live music. Eva would have liked to sing and play in Europe like her brother, Dan, but Annapolis proved to be a reasonable substitute. The atmosphere in the bars and restaurants had a certain Englishness and people liked to listen to well-played songs. Eva's guitar playing had much improved and it combined perfectly with her voice. For a small audience, watching an Eva Cassidy performance could be a meaningful musical event, not just someone with a guitar singing in the background.

"Russ from Annapolis" met Eva in a local pub in the city. He described his meeting with Eva in a comment left on the Eva Cassidy Yahoo webpage years later:

"It was an open mic night and a number of people were hanging out drinking beer, enjoying the music and waiting for their turn to play. Sitting at a table off to the side was a cute woman with a guitar leaning up against one knee. The place was fairly packed and since there was no one else at the table, I asked her if she would mind if I sat down. She said of course and I sat back to enjoy the music. A few minutes later, a friend who published a local music calendar came over to join me. He also knew the woman at our table and introduced me. She was pleasant enough but seemed kind of shy. I asked her if she was going to perform and she said she might, but still wasn't sure. She had just come from work and was somewhat grungy and said that she might just go home and take a shower instead. We talked about her work and when it was her turn to play she seemed reluctant to go onstage. She said that she had a couple of songs in mind but wasn't sure of what she wanted to play. I told her she could play whatever came to her heart and that if anybody didn't like it to tell them to go to hell.

"The crowd was acquainted with who she was and gave her a warm welcome. She took out her guitar, apologised for her appearance and started to play 'People Get Ready'. The crowd was so captivated you could hear a pin drop. She followed with 'Fields Of Gold'. When she finished the whole place exploded in a thunderous applause as she made her way back to the table."

Eva liked to play at the small, homely and intimate Maryland Inn. It was built in 1772 on Drummer's Lot where the town drummer would cry the daily news. The rules of the old inn are still prominently displayed, "No thieves, fakirs, rogues or tinkers. No skulking loafers or flea-bitten tramps. No slap an' tickle o' the wenches. No banging o' tankards on the tables. No dogs allowed in the kitchen, no cockfighting. Flintlocks, cudgels, daggers and swords to be handed to the innkeeper for safe-keeping. Bed for the night 1 shilling. Stabling for the horse 4 pence." Eva liked to play there because the audience really listened. Tape recordings from the Maryland Inn would later appear on Eva's 2000 album *Time After Time*.

Eva's shyness remained a problem, especially for those who didn't know her well. She lost herself completely in her singing, her voice alone transporting the listeners – she would look at the ground constantly, very rarely making eye contact with her audience. For this reason, Eva liked to play in dark and somewhat dingy bars and restaurants.

Pearl's was a small dark restaurant in a strip mall across the street from a cemetery. Punters ate in total silence when Eva performed and she felt safe because she wasn't hindered by spotlights.

Several live recordings were made at Pearl's and appeared initially on the 1994 bootleg album *Live At Pearl's*. They would later be included in various combinations on the albums *American Tune* (2003), *Somewhere* (2008) and *Simply Eva* (2011).

Reynold's Tavern is the oldest tavern in Annapolis and one of the oldest in the United States. Eva played here on Friday, October 7, 1994 with Dan and their friend Larry Melton. Everyone who saw it still talks about the performance today and agrees it was her best ever. Dan remembers: "There were some students in the audience so I was a bit worried that they would talk during this performance. But from the moment Eva began to sing they first whispered softly and then became completely silent in total admiration." Jackie Fletcher said about this performance: "When Eva, Dan and Larry played together the pure sound of all their instruments was extraordinary... no distortion, no equipment... Eva may have had a mic, but otherwise, they were all acoustic, if I remember correctly."

In the audience that night was Hugh Cassidy, who perhaps realised for the first time in his life how good his children really were. They had the potential to become really great. If the trio had recorded an album they would have been a hit in Europe. Eva exuded happiness – she was calling the shots on their set list, and being in that small dark brick-walled basement room, onstage with her brother and her best friend and surrounded by friends and family, gave her enormous comfort. There was a special and unusual chemistry between the three musicians that night and this spirit of love and affection was reflected in the audience. Dan and Larry's excellent musicianship enhanced Eva's performance, bringing it to a new level.

The assured performance was even more astounding when you learn that just before they had taken to the stage, Eva learned of the suicide of an old friend, Danny Gatton, a Washingtonian guitarist who fused rockabilly, blues, jazz and country into his own innovative style of playing. Dan and Eva had both taken several lessons with Gatton in 1984 and he had sat in with Eva during one of her Maryland Inn performances. Eva's voice can be heard on two songs they recorded together, 'Ain't That Peculiar' and 'Stand By My Side', both of which appear on the 1998 album *Untouchable*. Gatton never achieved commercial success, but peers such as Eric Clapton, Steve Earle, Willie Nelson and Les Paul have praised his fantastic musicianship. On October 4, 1994, Gatton locked himself in his garage in Newsbury, Maryland and shot himself. Dan and Eva were shocked to hear that he had taken his own life. "It feels like we have lost an uncle," Eva told her brother.

The gig at Reynold's Tavern was typical of the kind of show Eva was hoping to take to Europe. She loved small venues and wanted to perform her choice of songs in front of quiet and attentive audiences. Sadly, no one was there to capture the legendary show that night and Europe would prove to be a very long way off.

Chapter 9

Live At Blues Alley

Eva continued to work in the studio. Proving her versatility, in October 1995 she sang background vocals on a track for Tupac Shakur's album *All Eyez On Me.* The song was never released, but the voices of Eva Cassidy, Dr. Dre, Snoop Doggy Dog and Shakur came together on this recording.

Chris and Al needed a Plan B. If the major record companies weren't interested in the idea of Eva Cassidy making a studio album under her rules, why not record a live album themselves? They convinced Eva of the need to make such an album and decided they would record a performance in legendary jazz club Blues Alley. Aunt Isabel, Hugh's sister, gave Eva $1,000 towards the recording. They hired an engineer to record two performances, two different sets on two successive evenings – January 2 and 3, 1996. This would give them the opportunity to play each song twice if they needed to. Bryan McCulley, Eva's friend and colleague from Behnke's Nursery, would also film the performances but only 'What A Wonderful World' ended up on the subsequent DVD. Bryan had, in fact, fallen for Eva and had taken her to an Ozzy Osbourne concert in 1986, but she wasn't interested in a romantic relationship with him although they remained friends throughout her life. Remarkably, the film he took the second night of Eva singing her version of the *Wizard Of Oz* classic 'Over The Rainbow' would bring her world fame many years later. The DVD, *Eva Cassidy Sings*, released in 2004, contains more of this rare concert film – the only footage that has ever been released of Eva.

The burden on Eva to record the live album was heavy; she loved to work in a recording studio and she found live performance tough. This would also be her first real album with the band, making things even more difficult. However, Al and the band were convinced that she could do the job: they had never heard Eva sing badly or out of tune.

During rehearsals that same afternoon sound engineer Roy Battle discovered a strange noise. The sound mixer shared an electrical circuit with the light dimmers, so that when the lights were dimmed the electronic resistance increased, affecting the sound. Usually this low-level interference wouldn't be too intrusive on large speakers but on sophisticated recording systems the growling drone becomes all too obvious. Roy worked out what was causing the sound to distort and changed several cables. However, the first guests had started to arrive by then and the Blues Alley staff asked him to finish up. Believing it to be fixed, Roy gave the go ahead.

Eva had listened to Al carefully: she was decked up like a beauty queen and she paced around her dressing room in unfamiliar high heels. Al introduced the band, saying: "I want you to know that this is recorded live tonight. It's gonna be heard all over the world. And if you want to tell people, 'Hey, that's me right there!' you know, you've got to make noise in all the right places. So let's start it out right now and give a Blues Alley welcome to Miss Eva Cassidy!"

Private film footage shows the band taking to the stage, with the wall behind looking old and worn, and the Blues Alley logo prominently visible. The band members make a relaxed impression. Nobody seems to be aware of the technical catastrophe hanging over their heads.

Immediately after the first night's performances the group listened eagerly to the tapes. They soon realised that the problem with the sound had not been fixed at all, in fact there was something radically wrong with it. The entire recording had been in vain. Using the material for a record was out of the question.

This was a huge disappointment, not only because they had played very well that evening, but because the pressure for the second night was ratcheted up several notches. Making a live recording is always risky, musicians play more carefully than usual and every band member becomes acutely aware of their limits. Organising two sessions had helped them to relax on the first night: they had been fresh and eager and able to push the demands of recording live out of their minds.

On the second night of filming Bryan had changed his position to a seat in the back row, or maybe he had zoomed out with his camera. The entire band was feeling enormous pressure. We see Eva on the stage from head to toe, wearing a large oversized shirt, black leggings and work boots – there was no point dressing up, since everything rested on a decent audio. The smile on her face has transformed into worry. Her eyelids are heavy and she has dark circles under her eyes. Eva had developed a cold and everyone began to wonder whether she'd be able to cut it.

Once again Al introduces the band: "Let's have a warm Blues Alley welcome for Miss Eva Cassidy." Unusually, Eva announces the first song: "Gonna start off with an old Etta James song," she tells her audience. "She has a really good book out about her life... you should read it – it's juicy!" Eva's voice is audibly raw and she is unable to reach all the high notes, but she hides her vocal problems well; hearing Eva Cassidy sing with a cold is preferable to hearing anyone else in perfect health.

Agonisingly, they were plagued by further problems. The drums were too loud, which didn't trouble the live audience, but on the recording Raice was too forceful and it was not possible to tone him down in the mix. The engineer had closed all drum mics, but the other open microphones on the small stage had picked up the drums. The guitar, on the other hand, was too quiet. Keith did some marvellous things that night, but you have to listen closely to pick up his inventive fills and solos.

However, it wasn't all lost and they had enough quality material to fill the album, which they'd call *Live At Blues Alley*. Lenny Williams on his Steinway six-foot grand piano was brilliant. His hammer playing filled out the band's sound and he brought a jazzier feel to the music. In fact, thanks to Williams' swing style the number of jazz-influenced songs on this album is greater than any other by Eva. While this worked well on most of the album, the combination of guitar and piano on some of the ballads sadly diminishes their subtlety.

The delicious swing tempo of opener 'Cheek To Cheek' builds up from almost nothing, just Eva's finger-snapping and *a cappella* singing. She seems to be enjoying the moment, although she is not overly exuberant, and closes her eyes, losing herself in the music. In hindsight, it is easy to attach poignancy to many of the songs, perhaps most notably the phrase 'I'm in heaven'. We see the virtuous Lenny Williams playing his piano solo, his ears uncovered, a bit student-like in his small glasses. Lenny sings while playing his solo but unfortunately we can't hear him. A good example of how Eva became immersed in jazz on stage, at the end she makes a few piano-playing gestures with her hand to indicate how important Lenny's role is. The climax in the bridge lifts Eva's version above those released by other artists, Raice McLeod's drums swinging heavily, the volume high but not annoyingly so. Lenny provides the finishing touch with a top-rate piano solo. When the song is finished she mentions his name.

Eva's versatility enabled her to sound black and bluesy, her recording of T-Bone Walker's 'Stormy Monday' having fooled Chuck Brown into thinking she was a black singer. She had been nurturing this influence since she was a teenager, as a recording of Eva at 16, made by her old friend Ned Judy, reveals. By the Blues Alley performance, Eva has perfected the style, which makes you wonder what she would have sounded like 15 years down the line. The performance of 'Stormy Monday' is a real goosebumps moment, with Eva putting everything she has into the lyrics. She plays the white Fender Stratocaster on the song but defers to Keith for the guitar solo, which is majestic. He isn't showing off – this is superior craftsmanship.

'Bridge Over Troubled Water', chosen by Eva herself, is played in a very controlled manner with the two separate guitars easily distinguishable from one another. Keith solos accurately, seldom using his effects pedals and tuning instead to Eva's voice. A disadvantage of the live recording is that it leaves you wondering what Eva would have done with a second, third or even fourth part. Simon & Garfunkel's greatest asset was their harmonies, which are missing here, and a handful of backing singers might have solved the problem. Chris Biondo's bass playing stands out in this performance.

Billie Holiday's blues number 'Fine And Mellow' is tackled in a swing style, Chris' walking bass leading the way. Raice swings but fills in rather too much, and the piano accompaniment is a bit soft. During Lenny's solo the rest of the band holds back, and Eva can actually be heard commending Lenny to the audience. There can be no question that her confidence is on the rise, that she has made solid progress in finding her feet onstage. Keith also receives a round of applause, encouraged by Eva. But as a whole this song fails to convince.

The Eva Cassidy Band played songs best performed by a group of musicians as opposed to solo. Curtis Mayfield's 'People Get Ready', for instance, is dependent on the build-up of tension. The chord progressions would have been too simple to captivate an audience in a solo performance, although Eva's solo version on her 2011 album *Simply Eva* is great. In the *Live At Blues Alley* version Keith has the lead and Lenny Williams plays second fiddle. The performance is filmed in widescreen and the colour film is distorted to black and white because of the poor lighting. Finally we get a glimpse of drummer Raice McLeod. Keith's semi-acoustic jazz guitar can be heard via a Fender amplifier.

Eva possibly chose the Irving Berlin jazz standard 'Blue Skies' because of the lyrics, "No blue days but only blue skies from now on," a distant echo of the lyrics in 'Over The Rainbow'. It is an uplifting song, but the melody is too predictable.

Eva had found the courage to perform several solo pieces during the second night at Blues Alley. She can be heard to say: "This is what I listened to when I was a little, little girl. My parents had this record and I listened to it over and over again. I've wanted to do this song for a very long time. It's called 'Tall Trees In Georgia'." To see and hear Eva introducing a song is an exciting experience in itself for most fans. She twirls a button on the top of her semi-acoustic guitar. The guitar part is far from easy. In fact, this has to be played by a complete orchestra to get the right feel, but Eva catches the rhythm. Songs such as this demand the attention of the audience, something Eva didn't enjoy often enough playing in small and mostly noisy venues. The line "I don't wanna be any man's bride" has a poignant ring.

'Fields Of Gold' was Eva's best-known song during this period. Eva sang and played this ballad largely on her own, with Keith strumming his guitar intermittently. Written by Sting, former lead singer of The Police, who played it with a clear underlying beat, the song was performed by Eva as a ballad, evoking some long-lost timeless composition. Minus the applause, this version of 'Fields Of Gold' became the opening track to the 1998 compilation album *Songbird* and for many listeners it was their introduction to the hypnotic voice of Eva Cassidy – a perfect beginning that came sadly too late.

'Autumn Leaves' can be as simple or as complicated as you wish; it's one of the most beautiful and successful melodies ever composed. Eva chooses the most difficult option – the slowest version possible in which there is nowhere to hide, and the clarity of her delivery shows that she is confident, sure of her own skills. What follows is a mature and controlled version of the song. Halfway through we hear a piano solo from Lenny, there to keep Eva company. Eva seems to enjoy the performance and the film shows her glancing at him during his solo. 'Autumn Leaves' is a hugely popular, much-recorded song and in their simplicity it is easy to overlook the pathos in the lyrics. What makes Eva's version so impressive is that the changing of the seasons becomes almost tangible as she sings.

'Honeysuckle Rose' returns the set to a swing beat, with Lenny and Keith treating the listeners to genuine jazz solos. The build-up sounds thoughtfully arranged; the piece begins small with a walking bass and guitar but by the end the band spares no expense. During Lenny's solo somebody's head obscures the view. Keith clearly enjoys his one-two with Lenny.

The best song on the album is Al Green's 'Take Me To The River'. Thanks to 'Over The Rainbow' many of her fans have come to regard Eva as a ballad singer, but here is evidence that the often robust, high-tempo music of The Eva Cassidy Band could be genuinely irresistible. It is as if Eva has cast away all her worries as she throws herself into an energetic song that celebrates the pure joy of living. Chris Biondo slaps his funky bass and he retains a firm grip on the pulse. Keith knows exactly which high notes to hit in order to add the right ornamentation, making this song rock far more than others in the set. Eva sings as if she is Janis Joplin incarnate, downing a bottle of whiskey before a charismatic outburst. Lenny proves that he is also a beast on keyboards.

"I dedicate the next song to my mom and dad," says Eva, introducing 'Wonderful World'. Someone, probably Chris Biondo, repeats, "Mom and dad!" Hugh and Barbara were both present on that second night. Eva continues: "My Daddy taught me to play guitar." Despite her complicated relationship with her father, Eva is very gracious to him on this, her first live recording. 'What A Wonderful World', one of Eva's personal favourites, was the only song on the DVD of the first night at Blues Alley. Looking meaningful as she sings, Eva's eyes are lined in black kohl pencil and she is wearing a fine black blouse. The camera swerves amateurishly to the left to a dark emptiness and back to Eva again. The opening is quiet with guitar, bass and sweeping brushes. Eva's voice dominates easily and she is able to measure her emotions. When Keith plays his solo it takes a while before the camera finally alights on him in his stylish black suit with a pink tie. He is playing a Gibson ES-335 with a zebra-striped strap; his hair is somewhat thin and he is wearing large glasses and a fashionably trimmed beard.

The camera pans back to Eva as she sings, through two microphones, with her eyes largely closed and a wrinkle on her forehead. After the song she accepts her applause gracefully and in her gratitude she adopts the same expression on her face as her mother Barbara would have done. She would sing it again several months later at The Bayou, the last time she would ever perform the song in public. 'Wonderful World' gained a second life when the Georgian-Irish-English singer Katie Melua recorded it as a posthumous duet with Eva, giving the song new meaning and an even deeper poignancy.

At the end of the show Eva comes back to the mic: "Thank you so much for coming. You've been really wonderful." Ringmaster Sharon Shapiro can be heard to shout: "Eva Cassidy!" and there is further applause from the audience.

The final song on the album, Pete Seeger's 'Oh, Had I A Golden Thread', is a studio recording. Hilton Felton Jr., who played for Chuck Brown's Soul Searchers and Hughes Memorial United Methodist Church, plays Hammond B-3 organ, which gives the song a gospel feel even though the words lack any real spirituality. Eva reaches all the high notes very easily but the lyrics don't call for such a climax, and three-quarters of the way through there's an inescapable feeling of, "That's enough Eva, we know you can do it." This recording appears as little more than a showcase for Eva's ability to belt out a tune.

Several of the performances that were filmed that night did not make an appearance on the album, but were interesting nonetheless. The last song on the DVD *Eva Sings* is 'Over The Rainbow'. Chris had already used the studio version of 'Over The Rainbow' on *The Other Side* (1992) and they wouldn't use this one again, so Eva was relatively relaxed on the live performance. This version is far from perfect, but every second of it is rooted in the integrity that Eva brought to her work.

'You've Changed' is not in widescreen, but returns to full colour. Eva's hair has a somewhat ginger glow and her cardigan turns out to be grey. She is also wearing a scarf around her neck. She looks sharply at something next to the camera. Suddenly the camera zooms out again and picks up a shot of the complete Eva Cassidy Band minus Lenny. Raice, who now wears a beard, is clean-shaven and Chris plays on the left side of the stage on a white Fender bass.

'Time After Time', a solo piece, offers a big impression of a real artist at work with Eva putting maximum effort into her guitar solo.

A week later Al, Chris and Eva listened to the tapes to decide the running order of the album. Al and Chris did most of the talking as usual, with Eva listening intently. Suddenly from nowhere Eva spoke: "I don't like this." Al and Chris immediately tried to reassure her, knowing that it had been an expensive endeavour for Eva, paid for mainly out of her modest Behnke's salary and the revenues from *The Other Side*. "It's a live recording, Eva – listeners don't expect everything to be perfect." Chris tried to focus on each song, rather than the concert as a whole. But Eva's reply was an uncompromising "No".

They talked for hours and Eva was clearly tired after a long day at Behnke's. Al concluded: "It is possible to put together a good album out of the material we have." Chris added, "I can fix any glitches." Eva hesitated. Finally Chris and Al promised her that they would add some studio recordings to the live concert performances, which would lead to an acceptable and coherent album. Eva reluctantly agreed.

Eva asked her old friend Larry Melton, who was not only her first bass player but also a professional photographer, to take the cover photo for the proposed album. Eva and Larry drove to Georgetown and asked the owner of Blues Alley if he would put the announcement for Eva's concert back on the board above the entrance, to which he happily agreed. Eva is clearly completely at ease in Larry's photo – a depiction that would become one of the best-known images of her. Her guitar case lies on the ground, she leans casually against the doorway and the famous Blues Alley façade is prominent in the foreground.

In the sleeve notes Eva offers a slightly odd acknowledgement to "Jackie Fletcher for not making me buy sugar". In the context of the lyrics to 'Honeysuckle Rose' it is possible to conclude that this is a veiled declaration of affection, but of course it may also simply refer to Jackie having persuaded Eva not to take sugar in her tea as she was beginning to have a weight problem. Jackie reacts: "It was kind of silly that she put that writing into the liner notes. It was about how when we were housemates, and shared a kitchen, that I tried to tell her that she need not buy sugar – because I had lots of it in store... that's all! It fit into the lyrics of 'Honeysuckle Rose', I believe, and made sense to her. Thus the liner notes. I was very appreciative to appear in [them], but it was very, very silly."

Once the album running order was finalised, the next step was to try to sell it. Al Dale drove to all the record stores he knew with boxes of the album in the back seat of his car. He was able to leave one, two or at most three copies at each store, which was a good beginning. To promote the album The Eva Cassidy Band gave a few short performances. On July 6 they played at Tower Records in Washington, D.C., and a few days later at a Borders bookstore in Northern Virginia. Eva had completely forgotten to bring a box of CDs as she had promised.

Despite a positive review from Joel E. Siegel in the *Washington City Paper*, which stated "*Live At Blues Alley* is a triumph!", Eva's dissatisfaction with the album was clear in a letter she wrote to her brother, dated May 12, 1996: "I am already very aware of all the mistakes, being very critical, and I am my own worst critic and I have never needed Dad or anyone to tell me what is bad or wrong. This recording was incredibly stressful. We were having technical difficulties. My voice was in bad shape. It is always like that in the winter. I prefer studio recordings. I am so tired of competing with loud guitars and drums and I'm tired of singing R&B and blues. I'm really heading in the folk direction, yeah, folk with influences of any beautiful music – I'm sick of shouting. You will be laughing at how out-of-tune the guitars are on 'Fields Of Gold'. I spent about $4,000 on this CD. Aunt Isabel was kind and donated $1,000, but CD, taxes, dental work – two root canals and crown – new apartment, car insurance, has taken away all my savings and almost all of my credit card limit. But I'm still afloat – knock on wood. Now I hope I can sell my CDs and tapes and be doing OK. Love, Eva."

Eva performed again at Fleetwood's in Alexandria. The week before she had met Mary Ann Redmond and they had agreed to duet together. Bruce Lundvall of Blue Note Records was also present. Mick Fleetwood joined Eva onstage again and after the show he told Lundvall that he would be happy to play the drums on Eva's first Blue Note album. The president of the famous jazz label reacted with careful optimism.

Beneath the excitement that surrounded the release of the live album, the optimism of Chris Biondo and the enthusiasm of stars like Mick Fleetwood, it was becoming increasingly clear to everyone around Eva that there was something seriously wrong with her health. Later that week she visited a hospital for tests. She was rather laconic about it, but the results gave reason enough to be worried. Eva's doctors advised her to rest and to treat her health problems seriously, leaving her little chance to promote her own CD.

It was around this time that Eva told her mother that if she were to die she wouldn't have any regrets, because she had always been allowed to create.

Eva preferred to wear oversized clothes. (Ron Sachs/CNP/Corbis)

Eva jamming with Chris Izzi, Larry Melton and Joe Knaggs. (Ron Sachs/CNP/Corbis)

In 2002 Chris Biondo and his girlfriend Eileen White discovered five undeveloped rolls of film.
In each of the images Eva is depicted connecting with the elements of nature: water, earth and air.
Eileen used these photographs for the design of American Tune. (Courtesy Chris Bondio)

Eva and Chris in front of the Glenn Dale Studio.
(Courtesy Chris Bondio)

Eva on the beach in the Virgin Islands in 1993.
(Courtesy Chris Bondio)

Recent picture of Hugh and Barbara Cassidy. (Ron Sachs/Rex Features)

Eva playing her **Songbird Guild guitar.** (Matthew Dols)

Eva singing 'Over The Rainbow' during the Wammies Ceremony at the Hilton Hotel in Washington DC in 1994. (Adam Traum © Mike Schreibman)

Chris Biondo and Eva Cassidy at the Hard Rock Cafe, Washington DC in 1993. (Maria Fatima Villafana)

Three members of the metal band Kage presenting Eva her 1994 Wammie award for Female Vocalist in the category of Roots Rock/Traditional R&B. Kage is a four-piece group from the northern Virginia area, they received the 1993 Wammie awards for Artist/Group and Recording in the metal category for their album 'Change of Seasons.' (Adam Traum © Mike Schreibman)

Eva in the lounge of the Apollo Theater Recording Studio, New York.
This was in the same building as the Apollo Theater in Harlem. (Courtesy Chris Bondio)

Chris Biondo and Chuck Brown in Chris' studio in Rockville. (John Shore)

Chuck Brown in front of Blues Alley in an Eva Cassidy pose. (John Shore)

Photos of Eva from the 1991 session with Al Dale that were taken for use on a future album or as promotional posters. Eva was ambivalent about the results and requested that only her face from the images, not her body, would be used. (Norman Watkins)

Chapter 10

Truly, This Was A Voice From Heaven

Eva was a loyal friend and she reaped loyalty in return. Even after she had called off their romantic relationships, Chris, Mark and Ned's love for Eva did not fade; in fact, it seemed to many that their feelings for her intensified, taking on almost spiritual proportions.

Chris had moved on romantically. He met a girl called Eileen White, who would go on to play a role in designing the covers of several of Eva's albums. Initially Eva felt a bit uncomfortable when she was introduced to Eileen, but she soon realised that she wanted Chris to be happy and that maintaining a friendship with him was what mattered most of all.

Her relationships with women were usually less complicated, as there was no sexual pressure, but they could also lead to emotional confusion. Eva's closest bond was with her mother, Barbara, but at the age of 32 she needed some distance from her parents. Eva's best friend, Anna Karen, still visited her regularly. Eva was, in fact, quite possessive over Anna Karen, as she had been with Celia and Ruth in high school. She couldn't stand Anna Karen visiting Jackie and she showed both anger and jealousy if the two had fun together. Anna Karen was so important to Eva that she once remarked: "If Anna Karen had been a man I would have married her."

In 1995 Eva decided that it was time to take the next step and live on her own. Typically, she did not tell Jackie that she was house hunting as she was worried about upsetting her. Eva found an apartment not too far from Jackie's, although it was in a rather dangerous area of Annapolis. She left her former landlady a letter explaining that she had really enjoyed living with her but she now needed her own space and independence.

Jackie was a bit disappointed, but she understood perfectly well that Eva longed for her own home, her first. Jackie was concerned for Eva's safety, warning her to be careful and alert when she was out in her new neighbourhood. Despite the warning Eva was as determined as she had ever been and she moved in with her two cats. She came to an agreement with her new landlord that she would redecorate the flat in exchange for a month's rent. No one expected Eva to be able to keep her place clean, but to everyone's amazement she apparently did exactly that. This was a quality that no one had seen in Eva before. She was extremely proud of her small apartment and would allow nothing to stand in the way of the pleasure that independence might bring.

Anna Karen organised another surprise party for Eva's 33rd birthday on February 2, 1996, inviting all of Eva's friends for music and lots of fun. Eva felt more relaxed at this party and she stayed throughout rather than shutting herself away in her room. The highlight was inhaling helium from one of the many birthday balloons and answering the phone in a high-pitched "Smurf's" voice.

Jackie regretted Eva's moving out, but she was proud of what her former roommate had achieved: forging ahead with solo gigs, ending her unfulfilling relationship with Chris Biondo and growing more contented as time went by. For the first time in her life Eva was truly independent. Things could only get better and Eva's breakthrough as a singer would only be a matter of time. Jackie became Eva's unofficial manager and started by helping her to professionalise her methods of attracting new audiences. She called many of those who had seen Eva in concert, asking if they would like to come again. Later she would compile an email list to contact Eva's fans and promote her future gigs.

Things seemed to be going well for Eva on the work front as well. She had quit Behnke's and found a new job in Annapolis at Haven Studios, an art studio owned by Margaret Haven who designed and created murals for school cafeterias in the area. The work had two advantages: she could use her creativity and she was able to work on her own. Margaret soon discovered – like so many others – that even when working together, Eva could easily retreat into her own world and she would often eat her lunch in solitude. The only limitation was that Eva's work had to appeal to children – the rest was completely up to her. Eva's style had always been rather naïve and surreal, but positive, so this was the perfect job for her.

Most of the time they had to go about their work in the hot summer months while school was out, usually without the comfort of an air conditioner. They found all sorts of solutions to improve the conditions, such as using large floor fans, putting cold wet scarves around their necks or wearing baseball caps.

The process would begin with the two artists designing a scale drawing of the mural. Subsequently, these drawings would be transferred onto the wall at full size using a projector and paints. Eva was extremely good at painting coherent but playful pieces, even on the largest of walls. She not only had a stable, secure hand but she was also a fast worker.

The murals were sometimes several metres high and Eva often had to work on a ladder. She was often so focused on her work that she forgot to listen to her body and when her hip started to bother her, she put it down to her uncomfortable working position. Margaret Haven was worried about her talented employee and advised her to go back to the doctor. Despite her reluctance, Eva sensibly agreed, returning with the message that her pain had indeed been caused by working on a ladder for too long. The doctor had issued her with a pair of crutches and she drove for two hours to inform Margaret that she wouldn't be able to come to work that day.

Eva used these same crutches to walk to what would become her final gig, a performance at Jillians, a sports bar in Annapolis, in the final week of July 1996. It would turn out to be as disastrous as her debut all those years before, when her microphone had crashed to the ground. Eva had been drafted in at the last moment to substitute for another act that couldn't make it that evening. It was too late to ask her friends to come so only a handful were present. The rest of the punters played on jangling slot machines, downed their drinks at the bar, stared at the television or noisily racked up the balls on the pool table. Hardly anyone took much notice of the singer, who was forced to ask the proprietor to reduce the volume on the "pop crap" booming out in the bar. She had to rely on herself – there was no Chris Biondo to jest with the audience: "Are we playing too loud? Are you able to hear yourself talk?"

But Eva was relaxed – at least no one was looking at her. When her friends applauded she replied self-mockingly: "Thank you table one." There was, however, one barman who was frozen to the spot. When Eva's last notes evaporated into the smoky atmosphere of the obscure bar room he sighed and mumbled: "Truly, this was a voice from heaven."

The doctor was unable to offer a diagnosis for Eva's hip pain, but he advised her to stop climbing ladders. Nevertheless, she continued to show up regularly at Haven Studios to teach Margaret's other assistants. She much preferred being in the studio or in a school canteen to sitting at home, alone and in pain. Eva was finally discovering that she actually needed other people to be happy.

In August 1996 Eva fell in her bathroom while her parents were on holiday and she had to call Chris to help her. She hated going to the doctors and she tried to avoid going for as long as possible, but hiding was no longer an option. Chris took her to Johns Hopkins Hospital in Baltimore where they ran numerous tests and X-rays. It was at this visit that she discovered the seriousness of her condition.

Three years earlier she'd had a malignant mole removed from her back. She and her doctor had not linked this with the pain in her hip, but the X-ray showed a clear connection: the cancer had spread to her bones and her lungs. She was told that if she didn't take action she would have just four months to live. The only possible way to escape this fate was to undergo aggressive treatment. She would need a replacement hip, which had fractured, and start an immediate course of the strongest chemotherapy available.

Eva was faced with a terrible choice: she knew that the treatment would be difficult, but avoiding it meant certain death. She suddenly realised that she was desperate to live.

Before she embarked on the treatment she drove to Jackie's house to tell her how ill she was. Jackie tried to hide her tears. Eva comforted her, saying, "I'm not afraid to die." Jackie didn't know how to react and answered, "I'm glad that you are able to feel like that." Eva continued: "Do you know what the worst part is? I'm so worried about my mother... I don't want to hurt her."

With only a slight chance of improvement and very little of recovery, Eva started her chemotherapy on August 14, 1996. Unable to care for herself in her weakened state, she moved back into her parents' house. Over the gruelling weeks that followed she would lose weight, her hair would fall out and she would throw up constantly. But she never complained.

Eva's hip replacement surgery was set for August 21, 1996. After surgery she remained in hospital to recuperate. Many friends came to see her, leading to moments when her hospital room was too crowded, so she came up with the idea that every visitor had to create a work of art with paper and crayons before entering. In this way, her dreary hospital room was transformed little by little into an art gallery.

After her discharge she regularly visited Johns Hopkins for tests and chemotherapy, and while there Eva met a girl named Kimberley, who had been through chemotherapy once before. She also became friendly with Daniel, a former cellist for the Baltimore Symphony Orchestra. During the long waiting hours they discussed music and exchanged CDs. She told Daniel that she was working on a new album. The reality was that Eva was no longer able to record. She could no longer sing or play for long enough; her illness combined with the medication devoured her energy.

Chris Biondo arranged proper medical insurance for Eva, but several of Eva's friends felt the necessity to do something more, and Al Dale took it on himself to organise a concert at The Bayou, then the most prestigious club in Washington, D.C.

The members of The Eva Cassidy Band had been in deep shock since they'd learned of Eva's terminal illness: no one expected the adventure to end like this. Al Dale invited each of them to take part in the tribute, as well as Chuck Brown, Pieces Of A Dream and local acts such as Deanna Bogart, Tommy Lepson & The Lazy Boys, Al Williams, Keter Betts, Ron Holloway, Jr. Cline & The Recliners, Meg Murray, John Previti, Rich Chorné, Kevin Johnson, The Dave Elliott Band and Mary Ann Redmond. The intention was for the concert to become a tribute to one of the greatest talents Maryland had ever seen. The concert was named A Tribute To Eva Cassidy.

Watching the videotape of the Bayou concert is a moving experience. Few people have seen these images, because they have been kept largely private, with only small parts shown on an American ABC-Nightline documentary about Eva's life. Many years later the love and admiration for Eva is still visible, audible and tangible in these amateurishly filmed images. That night, Tuesday September 17, 1996, The Bayou was sold out. Eva's hardcore followers had mixed feelings about the turnout: where had all these people been when Eva needed their support as a struggling performer? But gratitude dominated. Eva would appear onstage that night. This might be the last chance to honour her and maybe even to hear her sing. Almost everyone who had meant anything to Eva during her short life was present that night.

Mary Ann Redmond, who had duetted with Eva several times, was the first to take to the stage. Next, Chris Biondo, Keith Grimes, JuJu House, Kent Wood and Chuck Brown entered. Sadly, Raice McLeod and Lenny Williams couldn't attend due to other commitments. The band played several jazz songs, Chuck Brown in his usual position as centre of attention. Unsure of whether Eva would be able to sing, the boys had chosen a flexible repertoire.

However, Keith Grimes then announced: "Ladies and gentlemen! Let's welcome to the stage... Eva Cassidy!" Carefully pushing her walking frame, it took Eva some time to walk onto the stage. She had clearly lost a lot of weight. She wore black leggings and a large men's shirt over a white T-shirt. Her velvet hat was flattering and concealed her hair loss. A shout was heard from the audience: "Eva, we love you!" Chuck adjusted the microphone stand down lower than usual.

The band started 'Red Top', a tune that Chuck would take lead in, but their arrangement made it possible for Eva to join in if she felt she could. She tried to add some backing vocals that became increasingly convincing as the song went on.

After 'Red Top' a sharply dressed representative of the local record industry entered the stage and addressed the crowd and Eva: "On behalf of the whole music industry I have the honour to present you with a gold CD." Eva was visibly moved by the surprise honorary award. Leaning on her walking frame, she looked much smaller than she was, her face very closely resembling her mother's.

The other musicians onstage consulted with Eva, she nodded and Keith picked up her guitar to hand to her. Before the concert it had been customised by guitar technician Mike Dove who had adjusted the strings so that Eva could strum them without too much strain. Chris Biondo moved a wooden stool with armrests behind Eva. He wrapped his arms around his former lover and lifted her courteously onto it. Eva smiled apologetically for her own helplessness. When the people in the audience noticed Eva's runny nose paper handkerchiefs were offered from all directions. Chris took one and gave it to Eva who patted her nose dry. "I had a shot of morphine before I came tonight," she explained. "That's what musicians do all the time, don't they?" In fact, Eva had actually stopped chemo some days before the concert to conserve energy for the performance. She played several introductory chords and continued to strum the opening part of 'Wonderful World'. Then she started to sing:

I see trees that are green red roses too
I watch them bloom for me and you
And I think to myself what a wonderful world

I hear babies cry I watch them grow
And they'll learn much more than I'll ever know
And I think to myself, oh what a wonderful world

The colours of the rainbow so pretty in the sky
Are also on the faces of the people passing by
I see friends shaking hands saying how do you do
But they're really saying I love you

I see trees that are green and red roses too
I watch them bloom for me and you
And I think to myself, oh what a wonderful world

The colours of the rainbow so pretty in the sky
Are also on the faces of the people passing by
I see friends shaking hands saying how do you do
But they're really saying I love you

I see trees of green and red roses too
I watch them bloom for me and you
And I think to myself what a wonderful world

Eva started hesitantly, but her voice held out and her accompaniment, though simple, was accurate. It was a miracle that Eva was able to play at all. As she sang Chuck left the stage as quietly as possible, unable to control his emotions. The same could be said for most of the people in the audience – everyone who was there was aware of the gravity of the moment. The members of The Eva Cassidy Band found it difficult to play, but they tried not to let their emotions overwhelm them. Chris Biondo avoided looking at Eva, his eyes completely focused on the neck of his bass guitar. Even professional keyboard player Kent Wood lost his way in this relatively simple arrangement: piano and guitar didn't mix well and it sounded like they were playing in different keys. The only person who was in control of the situation was Eva herself. She had tried in vain to record a number of songs in Chris's studio in the weeks prior to the concert. Now, with almost superhuman effort, she had really achieved something.

Several years earlier Eva had played the room at The Bayou with the band Method Actor in front of several Warner executives. On that night, everything had gone wrong. During her farewell performance on the same stage she displayed enormous character. She even found the courage to look each of the audience members in the eye when she reached the final line of the song: "I think to myself, what a wonderful... " – holding back, the expression on her face showed that she had finally come to realise how much all these people cared about her – " ... world.

Thank you so much, thank you so much!" She waved to her audience, laughed and waved again.

After the performance, Eva was taken to the balcony that the Warner hotshots had vacated nine years earlier. Now everyone present came to show Eva their love. She sat between her parents and seemed to enjoy all of the attention and unconditional love. "This is like a birthday party," she whispered to her mum. People embraced her and she embraced them back. When people cried Eva asked if they were all right.

'What A Wonderful World' had been Eva's public swan song. The Bayou concert raised $10,000. It was hoped that the money would allow Eva to travel or to make a CD. Instead she gave the money to four young cancer patients, including Kimberley and Daniel, whom she had met at Johns Hopkins.

Eva's dream had been to record a studio album under favourable but precise circumstances. But she and Chris had worked at too slow a pace and even then he'd had the anxious premonition that they would be too late. It's likely that Eva's delay in completing her work had something to do with her perfectionism; as long as your work remains unfinished no one can say that it isn't good enough. Dozens of half-finished recordings languished on the shelves of Chris' studio. "That is something we are going to work on later," they used to say. But as Chris tried desperately to finish the album that would be called *Eva By Heart*, it became increasingly clear that there would be no later.

After learning of his sister's serious illness, as soon as he was able, Dan flew to New York with Anna Karen and Blues Bar owner and friend Jonas Helgason in October. During that time there were no direct flights from Iceland to Washington, D.C. and they had to make the last part of their trip by train.

When Chris heard that Dan was back home he asked him to play a violin part in a song he and Eva had recently discovered. 'I Know You By Heart' is about a cancer patient who tragically loses the fight to the disease. It was composed by Diane Scanlon, who also recorded her own version. Dan felt a bit uneasy because the song was in the difficult key of A-flat, but he retuned his violin up a half-step to play in the more relaxed key of

G. He had to invent his own violin part, but Eva's vocals inspired him to reach a higher musical level. The lyrics of the song are very touching, the line "You left in autumn" turning out to be horrifically prophetic. Eva changed the line "I see your profile" to "I see your sweet smile".

After a day's work Dan brought the tape to Eva who by now was confined to her bed for the better part of the day. She was very happy with the result and reacted with her usual self-mockery, saying: "Your part is good."

'Love Heals The Wounds It Makes', later called 'Time Is A Healer', was also completed. Fellow singer Mark Carson was a church pastor and Eva loved his singing. The bass line was supplied by Larry Melton on double bass.

Eva was extremely satisfied with 'Wayfaring Stranger', one of the demos she had made for Blue Note Records. This version is entirely her own arrangement and she had instructed each of the musicians' parts.

'Songbird' was virtually a solo performance: Eva played most of the instruments herself, while Chris created the beat with a drum machine. She was thrilled with the result.

Eva had been determined in better days to record at least one song in a real Baptist-church gospel style. Coincidentally, gospel pianist Mark Carson knocked on the studio door at the exact moment they were recording 'How Can I Keep From Singing?' and was asked to join them. Anthony Flowers, a Baptist-church organist, provided an organ accompaniment. Dan added several violin parts which were doubled and tripled and a round of applause was added to the final track. Chuck Brown's "Thank You Lord!" was the icing on the cake.

Chris worked as fast as he could. He was desperate to have Eva authorise these versions because he longed to make a record that was 100 per cent in her spirit before she was lost to her illness. Sadly, time would prove to be tragically short.

Chapter 11

Give Yourself To Love

In the car on the way home from her final concert at The Bayou, Eva spoke to her parents about how she had touched her audience with the song 'Wonderful World'. At this late stage in her life, she had finally felt the adoration of an audience, something that had taken her a long time to understand. At 33 and on the border between life and death, it seems that Eva had finally been able to come to terms with who she was and bask in the warmth of an appreciative audience.

Although writing was far from easy, in the coming days she would send more than a hundred thank-you notes to everyone who had contributed to the success of the evening.

By October 1996 it was clear to everyone that Eva's illness was terminal. She spent most of her time in bed. On good days she was able to move but only in a wheelchair. When she had visitors she wore a baseball cap or a velvet beret. To distract her from the boredom, her friend Elaine Stonebreaker would take her to her favourite spot in the high grass along the canal on the south side of Alexandria.

After consulting with her doctors Eva's parents told her that further treatment was senseless. Her father was frustrated that she had refused to accept the reality of her illness, delaying for so long to seek proper treatment, and though desperate to put all their difficulties to rest, she felt unable to discuss it with him. Relying almost constantly on morphine and painkillers, she was in a near permanent slumber towards the end. She liked to have great chunks of ice placed on her tongue, which relieved her dry mouth. Hugh administered the medicine and helped her to eat and drink as much as he could. He wanted to show how much he loved his daughter.

When Bruce Lundvall at Blue Note heard how ill Eva had become he felt an overwhelming need to call her and apologise for not offering her a record deal. Eva was in a lot of pain, but her mother thought it important that the two talked. "I'm sorry Eva," Bruce said, "We should have made an album together. It's my fault. Forgive me, I have made a terrible mistake." Then he started to cry. Eva whispered: "It's all right. Don't worry. I don't have to forgive you, we had a nice contact. It's good that we have met." It was scant reassurance. Like all great record men, Lundvall made decisions on instinct, but in the case of Eva his instinct had forsaken him.

Eva's friends, including Anna Karen, dropped in on a regular basis. Eva liked to go outside in her wheelchair, but she no longer had the energy to rise from her bed. Anna Karen opened the window so that Eva could still look outside. Picnicking in the garden were Larry, Ned, Hugh and Dan who decided to play for Eva, improvising an old fashioned gypsy-swing set from under the window. Several songs in they could hear Eva humming. She was even able to give some musical direction.

In the last month of her life Eva received many visitors. It was tough on her ailing strength, but her friends really wanted to spend time with her. Larry Melton in particular struggled with the visits. He was lost for words by her bedside. It was as if her friends found it harder to say goodbye than she did. Chris Biondo could see that Eva found it difficult to deal with visitors who were distressed. From that moment on Barbara answered the phone, making the decision to limit visits.

Since Eva was too ill to leave the house Barbara thought it would be a nice idea to invite folk singer Grace Griffith to their home. Grace found Barbara's message on her answering machine: "My daughter Eva is very ill, and it's all terribly sad and Eva loves your singing and would appreciate it very much if you could come and sing for her." Grace immediately called back and made an appointment to visit the Cassidys with her friend and colleague Marcy Marxer.

When Grace and Marcy arrived Eva was sitting in her wheelchair in the living room, having summoned all of her strength to leave her bed. Dan, who had just finished his violin parts on 'I Know You By Heart', took part and Hugh joined them on his cello. It turned out to be a glorious autumn afternoon full of beautiful music. Eva was unable to play or even move but she used her last reserves of energy to sing with her "angel brigade", as she called them. Their voices like a heavenly choir, Grace, Marcy and Eva harmonised their collective repertoire of folk songs. Eva asked for 'My Heart's In The Highlands', a ballad by the Scottish poet Robert Burns, which they sang multi-parted, accompanied by Grace and Marcy's guitars, Hugh's cello and Dan's violin.

Farewell to the Highlands, farewell to the North,
The birth-place of Valour, the country of Worth;
Wherever I wander, wherever I rove,
The hills of the Highlands for ever I love.

My heart's in the Highlands, my heart is not here;
My heart's in the Highlands a-chasing the deer;
A-chasing the wild-deer, and following the roe,
My heart's in the Highlands wherever I go.

Farewell to the mountains high covered with snow;
Farewell to the straths and green valleys below;
Farewell to the forests and wild-hanging woods;
Farewell to the torrents and loud-pouring floods.

Together they created an ethereal, almost other-worldly sound. Barbara then made a request: "We are not sure whether Eva will still be with us at Christmas. Can we sing a Christmas song together?" She handed Grace and Marcy the lyrics of a song that she knew from her childhood: the German language version of 'Silent Night'. They sang the first verse in German and the rest in English. The Christmas carol about the birth of a child who would also die at the age of 33, was the last song that Eva would ever sing.

During Eva's final weeks she was visited by nurse and spiritual advisor Kathy Oddenino. Kathy's first impression of Eva was that she had been naive in her attitude towards her illness. Now, however, she was facing the truth and had become fearful of dying. She had many questions and wasn't afraid to ask them.

Kathy was able to gain an accurate impression of the kind of person Eva was. Eva told her spiritual guide about the happy moments she had experienced as a young girl. Her best memories were all associated with music: playing together and singing with her brother, sisters, father and mother. Eva spoke about the pain she had lived through at junior high, surrounded by uncaring teenagers and bullies. It was during her adolescence that Eva began to realise she was different to others. She could rely on her mother, Barbara, but since that painful period Eva had begun to believe that the body was unnecessary baggage and it was her spirit that carried her. She concluded that she had to die to reveal her true spirit.

Kathy came to believe that Eva's problems with self-esteem had started in her early childhood. As a little girl Eva was afraid to vent her opinion or to express her deepest thoughts. She thought a lot, she had a very creative mind, but she kept everything inside so that this bottling up of feelings became second nature to her. Eva's incapacity to express herself had everything to do with her fear of being judged.

Eva began to accept that holding back her emotions had caused much of the sadness and frustration in her life. She told Kathy how much she regretted discovering this too late. Eva found her spiritual balance in art and music. For her, the connection between the lyric and the music mattered and she found comfort in certain songs. She was able to immerse herself in her songs and bring happiness to others through her performances, but her inability to express emotion when it came to real life had hampered her. Eva was especially sad that she would no longer be able to reach out through her music. With time Kathy could have helped Eva to accept herself and move on from her complex emotions. But the sad truth was that there was no time left.

Eva sometimes compared her childhood friend Celia Murphy with Jesus because she had often helped her without ever asking for anything in return. The two were on the same spiritual level. Eva loved talking about angels and she hadn't shied away from the fact that in order to become an angel herself she must leave the earth first. Like everyone else, Celia found it very difficult to watch Eva during her last struggle and she felt the need to comfort her vulnerable friend with words from the Bible. Celia chose a reading from the book of psalms, Psalm 23: The Lord is my shepherd: *"Even though I walk through the valley of the shadow of death, I will fear no evil, you are with me; your rod and your staff, they comfort me. Surely goodness and love will follow me all the days of my life, and I will dwell in the house of the Lord forever."*

In the final week of October Anna Karen and Dan said their goodbyes to Eva. Anna Karen longed to say so much to her but she kept her final words light and breezy, mentioning new shoes and clothes. For Eva it didn't matter any more; she was happy with the energy she received from Anna Karen. They hugged and said "goodbye" to each other.

Then Dan entered the bedroom. "You are going ahead of us," he told his beloved sister. "We will miss you, but you are going to a place that is better than this one. Be brave, be strong." Eva answered: "You are really good. You are one of the best musicians I've ever played with. You can play with anyone."

Larry and Ned, who both had to return to LA, also said emotional farewells to Eva. Chris Biondo was the last of her friends to leave. He was there as Eva slipped into a coma. The room was chilly and Eva's parents had put on a CD of New Age "healing angel music". It was too much for Chris who apologised to Barbara as he left.

Towards the end Eva's parents increased her dose of the liquid morphine drug known as Breakthrough and she slept for a long time. When she woke up she asked to listen to her own music and watched TV for a few moments. After that she became drowsy again.

Eva's final visitor was Kathy Oddenino. She tried to encourage Eva with positive words, certain that the end was near.

Hugh and Barbara stayed awake in Eva's bedroom for the final two nights of her life. Eva Cassidy died just after midnight on November 2, 1996.

That night two of Eva's friends, Mark Merella and Anna Karen, both saw Eva appear to them. She told both that everything was okay and that the place where she was staying was wonderful.

On November 17, staff journalist Richard Harrington wrote a long article that appeared on the front page of the art supplement of the *Washington Post On Sunday*, entitled 'The Death Of Eva Cassidy Haunts Friends And Fans'. It brought home just how much Eva's music and voice would be missed. Harrison begins his article with a quote from Bruce Lundvall:

> *"Eva Cassidy had the most extraordinary and singular voice I had heard in a very, very long time," Lundvall says. "It was distinctive not only because of its power but because of its timbre when she sang quietly. It was so very mysterious – it would just freeze me. The first time I ever heard her was in my office. She sang an a cappella 'Amazing Grace' and I was just nailed to the wall. I made a very bad mistake. I should have signed her... She was a kid. Who knew?"*

Harrison described Eva Cassidy as a diamond, no longer in the rough but not yet in the proper setting that would showcase a voice so pure, so strong, so passionate that it should have found a home just about anywhere. "Cassidy could make anything – folk, blues, pop, jazz, R&B, gospel – sound like it was the only music that mattered." The article went on to say:

> *"Eva Cassidy is not a familiar name, even here in her hometown. She was a secret slowly exposed by word of mouth from those who stumbled into her world and emerged forever fans. It explains why so many musicians sought Eva Cassidy out. Everybody felt like she was a part of their mix. She was shy, of course. She was neither blessed nor burdened with the aggressiveness and ambition that fuel so many singers and musicians. But there was a spiritual solidity about Cassidy. She was determined, focused, strong.*
>
> *"I don't even think she knew how good she was," says Chuck Brown, the "Godfather of Go-Go", who made a much-acclaimed album of jazz and pop standards with Cassidy in 1992. "She liked the idea of possibly making a living off music, but if she never got a record deal or never became famous, she*

wouldn't lose any sleep over it," says Chris Biondo, Cassidy's producer and bassist. *"What's sad is that people were just beginning to figure how good she was when she got sick."*

"It wasn't just the music," says Biondo. *"Eva fought as hard as she did because she wanted to ride her bike again, to go out and spend Sundays with her mother.*

Her mother, Barbara Cassidy, says Eva *"was a very private person, with a sense of vulnerability about her when she sang. I think that's what touched people's hearts about her."*

Biondo's recording studio would ultimately be a bridge to a number of musical opportunities that Cassidy would never have sought out. She was raw talent. *"One of the reasons she got so good, whenever a song was on the radio, she would always sing with it – not the melody, always the harmony,"* Hugh says. *"She had a sense of harmony – it didn't matter what part – high, low, she could take any part. When they'd call her in to lay down tracks, she'd go in and just do it because she had an incredible ear."*

"Her voice projected her feelings, and I could feel everything she was singing. It's a devastating blow to lose her. I felt I'd been knowing her all her life," Chuck Brown reacted. Cassidy's singing with Brown, says her friend Jackie Fletcher, was *"simple and clear and gorgeous, the quiet crystal clear ballad interspersed with soulful blues tunes. It was not muddied in the water of rock-and-roll, and it made Eva work – she had to have power in her voice to sing with Chuck."*

"When I found out she was sick, I haven't been right since," says Brown, his voice choking up with emotion. *"I had to stop all of my recording sessions 'cause I just wasn't in no mood to go in the studios to do anything..."*

"She was scared to play in front of a lot of people," Biondo says, *"though she became more comfortable when she realised her singing really moved people."*

Singer Mary Ann Redmond, who shared several stages with Cassidy, says: *"Female singers are a rare breed – they can be insecure and a little bit catty and weird – but Eva didn't have any of those traits. She didn't have any ego, she just wanted to sing because she loved music. She didn't even really like being onstage that much – she'd rather sing background than be in the foreground."*

Nicky Scarfo, who produced gangsta rap at Biondo's studio – and sometimes enlisted Cassidy for backup vocals – couldn't understand why she wasn't a big star. "Chris said she didn't care at all, she just wanted to live her life peacefully. She was just happy doing what she did... There was no sense of urgency."

Like Dale and Brown, Scarfo's first reaction when meeting Cassidy was doubt. "It was: 'Chris, are you jiving?' But Eva got on that mike and just destroyed it, we didn't believe what we were hearing."

At first, Scarfo didn't think Cassidy would want to work in gangsta rap. "I had her sing a hook that said 'I want to thank you pimps and players' and I couldn't even imagine it – but the way she sang it, she made it sound good, you know!"

Scarfo laughs at the memory. "She just put a feeling and a touch on words that brought them across with soulfulness and jazziness all wrapped up into one. And the way she did harmonies is unbelievable. She could do four-part harmonies just like that – 1, 2, 3, 4, write it and hit it, all the harmonies, note for note, and be done in 20 or 30 minutes. It was unbelievable."

So was the rappers' reaction. "These are guys that would shoot me if I messed their tape up. When she'd come in," Scarfo says, "I swear, it was like the principal walking into a class, I've never seen them so respectful and well behaved. These guys were really devastated when they found out about Eva..."

"She didn't really understand that there were categories between songs; if they were ones she happened to pick, that was her category. I don't think until the day she died she ever understood what that was all about."

"Eva cared enough about it to try to get herself pumped up to get there," Dale says. *Effects of the still-spreading cancer and the harsh side effects of chemotherapy had made Cassidy so ill that she decided to forgo chemo on the two days before the show [at The Bayou]. When she arrived at the club – moving slowly with a walker, a sprightly beret masking the loss of hair – Cassidy looked frail but golden.*

"Eva had such a sparkle that night – she said, 'This is like my big birthday party.' It may have been the one time in her life that she came to terms with the idea that people really do like her and think that she's a terrific talent. It filled her to know people appreciated and loved her."

"I think that was the best day she had after she got real sick," Biondo says. "But she came home and threw up that night, she was in a lot of pain. The arm that she used to strum her guitar had cancer in it... "

Hours later, Cassidy was back at Johns Hopkins for chemo. According to Jackie Fletcher, "Her peak was The Bayou. She started sliding downhill that next morning. She lost so much of her strength over a short period of time and after that night, she was always in the wheelchair because of the pain and because her bones were so brittle."

Over the next few days, Cassidy tried to send thank-you notes to the performers and those who helped put the tribute together, even if she could only do one a day. The cards bore a heart with a smiling face.

"She liked songs with singable choruses," folk singer Marcy Marxer recollects. "Songs like 'Give Yourself To Love' and 'My Heart's In The Highlands'. Grace Griffith and I would sing, and she'd just jump in with the third part. Sometimes we'd have to sing softly to hear Eva, and she'd say, 'Let's make a nest' – and we'd circle up real close."

"I once heard Eva say she wasn't afraid of dying," says Al Dale. "She never even had a tear in her eye. It was always, 'Well, how you doing, Al?' You almost never got a chance to say 'Well, Eva, how are you doing?' She never even asked for anything – you could give her an apple and she'd think it was a diamond ring."

Barbara Cassidy remembers that earlier this year, Eva visited relatives in Nova Scotia and sat on some rocks watching meteors go by all night long. "She said it was so incredible. She loved different cloud formations, the way the sun would feel to her through the breeze, flowers. She just added so much beauty to my life... "

Maybe someday 'I Know You By Heart' will be released, its melancholy beauty heard by audiences around the world. Then, the song's sound may well bring tears to strangers' eyes, but right now it's the silence that hurts those who knew the singer.

Eva had begged of her parents: "Don't put me in a casket." And so her mother asked her, "What would you think of having your ashes scattered on the beach at St. Mary's Lake?"

On the same day that Richard Harrington's article was published two cars drove to a park outside of the town in St. Mary's County. In the first were Anette, her sister-in-law and their cousin Vivien. In the second were Chris and Barbara who sat in the front seat and on the back seat Hugh, Margret and Dan. When they arrived they wandered through the woods to the banks of St. Mary's Lake in St. Mary's River Watershed Park in the south of Maryland, the beautiful nature reserve that had been one of Eva's favourite spots for walking and swimming.

Eva was carried away like dust in the wind. Hugh read a poem that he had written some days before:

The colour, the radiance
You caused us to see
Would have been missed
But for your eye
That sought tranquility
In the Golden Time.

Child of the sun
Daughter of the One,
May you find your rest
In the Golden Time

It's ironic that Eva's love for the summer and sunlight was to prove fatal to her.

The Reverend Linda Olson Peebles visited Hugh and Barbara to discuss preparations for a remembrance ceremony for Eva, which was held several days after her ashes were scattered into the lake. Linda had never met Eva personally, but she knew her music. Linda is an acquaintance of Grace Griffith and they are both Unitarian Universalists.

Linda was not only a preacher but also a singer-songwriter. In the eighties and nineties Grace Griffith had organised open-mic evenings in her coffee house and Linda had played and sang there regularly. The family thought it important that a liberal female preacher who loved music speak at Eva's ceremony. Linda examined Eva's work, listened to stories and memories of Eva from Hugh and Barbara and followed their wishes for the service. Music was a core element to the Cassidys, so Chris Biondo was asked to bring his expertise and equipment to the ceremony.

The ceremony was held under an enormous canopy in a Maryland State Park not far from the city of Greenbelt. It was a sunny afternoon, relatively mild for the time of year. About 600 guests arrived. Family members who were present included Barbara, Hugh, Anette, Margret, Dan, cousin Dorothee, grandmother Clara, Aunt Isabel, cousins Laura and Vivien and several others.

Linda welcomed everyone to the celebration of Eva's life, commenting that the place was made holy by their being there. She expected it soon to be filled with laughter, tears, music and silence. Linda began by singing one of Eva's favourite songs *a cappella*, 'Give Yourself To Love', written by Kate Wolf:

> *Kind friends, all gathered here, there's something I would say:*
> *What brings us together here, has blessed us all today;*
> *Love has made a circle, that holds us all inside,*
> *Where strangers are as family, and loneliness can't hide.*
> *Give yourself to love, if love is what you're after;*
> *Open up your hearts to the tears and laughter;*
> *Give yourself to love, give yourself to love.*

Linda explained that Eva's influence would be felt as long as memory endured. She mentioned some of the highlights of Eva's short life: "Eva was an artist – visual artist all her life – decorated floors, murals, furniture; she was a vocal artist all her life – always recognised for her talents. She went to schools right around here – Highbridge Elementary in Bowie, Robert Goddard Junior High in Lanham, Bowie High School, PG Community College for a short time. She spent most of her life pursuing her music and living her art. One of her day jobs was working at Behnke's Nursery, working with plants – she had a deep love of nature.

"She always performed gigs, and sang with different groups. In the past years, her art came together and she has been acclaimed for her music. Her spirit and her voice won her awards and fans, and moved so many of us. She won Wammies, and will again be honored tomorrow night, as she is inducted into the Washington Area Music Hall of Fame. Someone told me Eva was the most talented person she'd ever met, but that talent was always held in a person that was modest, gentle and spiritual. Eva loved her music and her artwork and lived for them. She was a spirit who engaged in life and created beauty."

After Linda's introduction Dan played a solo piece, 'Scottish Lament', on his violin. Hugh's brother, John Cassidy, and friends Ruth Murphy and her husband Jim Dickey spoke some words. Celia Murphy sang 'Hearth And Fire' by Gordon Bok. Her brother Chris played guitar.

Al Dale, Eva's former manager, also spoke at the ceremony. Barbara had asked Chris Biondo to say something as well, but he was too overcome to go through with it.

Grace Griffith sang a song that meant a lot to Eva: Pete Seeger's 'Oh, Had I A Golden Thread'. Eva had recorded the song in the studio and it had been included on the *Live At Blues Alley* album. On the liner notes Eva described the song as her favourite. The melody was quite simple, a freer version of 'Nearer My God To Thee', but Eva was able to improvise the chords. The lyrics connected with Eva and the visual artist in her was attracted to the weaving of a rainbow design. To Eva, the rainbow was a symbol of a happiness that awaited her somewhere in the distance. Grace Griffith's version had a Celtic touch.

Reverend Peebles closed the ceremony by saying: "No person can sum up the life of another. Life is too precious to be passed over with mere words. Rather it must remain as it is remembered by those who loved and watched and shared. For such memories are alive, unbound by events of birth and death. And as living memories, we possess the greatest gift one person can give another. Treasure your memories for they are your way of keeping Eva with you, now that her physical presence is gone. For she truly enriched the lives she touched.

"Eva left us not just the gift of memories. She has left us the wonderful gift of her music. We will always be able to hear her voice and her soul in her recordings. She also left us the example of how special the power of creativity can be in our lives. Eva wrote on the liner notes of her *Live At Blues Alley* CD: 'Special thanks to the creative spirit that flows through everyone.' She lists many people who shared their creative selves and their love and encouragement with her. But she understood that we are all part of that creative spirit that flows through everyone. Eva felt the gift of life – in art and in nature, in people and in music. Thank goodness for Eva and her love and her sharing with us all.

"As we bring this service to a close, we do it with great thanks and rejoicing for the life we were blessed to know. Following our Benediction of blessing to each of you, the family will gather with glasses, and invite you to go to one of the refreshment tables to find a drink. We will with grateful hearts listen to Eva's own song and then offer up a toast in celebration of her life. Many of us will feel her most closely when we listen to her music. Her music heals. Eva has received letters from fans who told of how her music companioned them through difficult times or helped old wounds begin to heal. Perhaps it is Eva's music that can best turn our sadness today towards the joy and celebration she would want us to feel today."

The songs that were played at the gathering that day were those that Chris had finally completed for the album *Eva By Heart.*

Fifteen years later Rev Linda Olson Peebles looked back on the life of Eva Cassidy and concluded: "Eva's religion was the power of the Spirit as it comes through people in music or art, expressed in love and in nature. She was not a creedalist, did not adhere to one particular branch or denomination or faith tradition; her spirituality was one of openness and universality, reverence and joy for the whole of creation, and for all of us who are part of it.

"Songs were her prayers. Many people find comfort in Eva's interpretations of gospel songs. Eva also found strength in singing them. I cannot say exactly how we should interpret what they meant to her, however. I don't think she was a person who felt that being Bible-centred was important to her faith; nor did she believe that Jesus was the only way. The family didn't ask for any reference to Christ in the service. For Eva, the power of the gospel songs was in their universality to all peoples' experiences, that in the face of hardship or sorrow, life and love are capable of carrying us and comforting us."

★

At the next Wammies award ceremony Hugh and Barbara were presented with several awards on behalf of Eva, who was chosen as Artist of the Year. Chris, the other band members and Grace Griffith were present and they talked with Hugh and Barbara about releasing the posthumous studio album *Eva By Heart*. Since Eva had received the highest accolade at the awards ceremony, the chance to create a successful record had finally arrived.

Chapter 12

Songbirds Keep Singing

All of those who belonged to the close circle around Eva reacted to her death in their own way and did everything they could to keep her flame burning. Hugh Cassidy tried to cope with the loss of his daughter by making a statue of her. He had been making sculptures from an early age, but it wasn't until Eva died that Hugh really became absorbed in creating art from scrap metal. He must have been inspired because the face of the angel he designed has Eva's features. Like Eva, Hugh makes realistic human faces with a surreal twist, yet there's always hope in the work. The Cassidys' art isn't necessarily cheery, but it is usually positive.

In 1997 Chuck Brown recorded an album of jazz standards called *Timeless*, which he released in 1998 and dedicated to Eva. It was produced by Lenny Williams and Chris Biondo who both played in the jazz combo as well. Chuck didn't want to perform with another female singer again. He said about his former companion: "There will never be a new Eva."

Eva's friend Anna Karen sent the recording of 'Fields Of Gold' to its writer, Sting. The former Police singer had rarely heard a voice of such purity. He was sorry to learn of Eva's death and believed that this somehow took the song to a deeper emotional level. He was moved by

Eva's version of his song: "Her voice has a magical quality. It suggests something ethereal – something unattainable," he said in an interview with Richard Harrington of the *Washington Post* on March 23, 2001.

It was a very sad time for everyone. Chris Biondo knew that to really honour Eva he had to finish *Eva By Heart* and in doing so create an album from the best material available. Working day and night on it comforted him. The gospel song 'Wade In The Water' was particularly soothing. The line "God's gonna trouble the water" refers to the healing scene in John 5:4: *"For an angel went down at a certain season into the pool and troubled the water, whosoever then first after the troubling of the water stepped in was made whole of whatsoever disease he had."*

Up to that point Chris had managed to record the acoustic guitar, bass, drums and vocal parts. But Eva would certainly have liked a muted trumpet solo in their version, so he invited Chris Walker, an excellent trumpeter, to play it. Eva hadn't been satisfied with her own chorus part so Chris asked a handful of musicians, Troy W-D Brown Sr., Eric D Dorsey, Dontane Lane and Bryan Roberts, who were recording their own material in the studio at that time, to sing several background parts.

The last song Eva recorded was 'The Water Is Wide', which was titled 'Waly, Waly' on the album. It is a sad traditional based on the story of Lady Barbara Erskine, who married the second Marquis of Douglas in 1670 but was falsely accused of adultery by a former lover. Chris wasn't initially fond of the tune or the recording they had, but since it was one of Eva's favourites he agreed, as a gesture of respect, to put it on the album.

They had originally intended to use the recording on *Live At Blues Alley*, but that proved unsatisfactory so Chris had his work cut out. First he removed Eva's vocals and gave the two parts to Lenny Williams, who composed a new score digitally using Celtic drums, cymbal swells and strings. The song opens and closes with the sound of rolling waves, wind and seagulls. Even a harp, artificial bagpipes and an electronic oboe can be heard in the distance. 'Waly, Waly' is now one of Chris' favourite tracks.

'Blues In The Night', by Harold Arlen and Johnny Mercer, was finished, but Chris knew that Eva would have preferred real strings to the keyboards they had on the track. Karen van Sant from the Kennedy Center Opera House Orchestra happened to be a keen Eva fan and she offered to help Chris. She listened to the song a few times and played several violin parts. Chris then layered these until he had a complete violin orchestra. The wind instruments still sound slightly artificial, especially if you bear in mind how fond Eva was of performing with a real big band. Strangely enough, the horns begin to sound more realistic later in the song. Eva's parts are layered into a choir and although her singing is slightly forced her pronunciation sounds really black: "My momma done tol' me when I was in pigtails."

Mertis John Jr's much-covered 'Need Your Love So Bad', a posthumous duet with Chuck Brown, had originally been a solo piece. Chris faded several of Eva's parts down to allow Chuck to duet, with convincing results. Eva and Chuck's voices are like yin and yang, each the other's perfect counterpart. At the end of the song Chuck ends with: "Love you Eva". It took many sessions to complete because Chuck was still so emotional; he really loved Eva and missed her dearly. The horn parts on the track were played by musicians drafted in from several local military jazz bands, including Chris Walker and Leigh Pilzer, who had played on the Chuck and Eva album *The Other Side*.

'Say Goodbye' was written exclusively for Eva by composer Steven Digman, who lived in Rockville, not far from Chris' studio. The song was far from finished when Eva died – they had managed to record her guitar, the bass and drum parts. Chris got Keith Grimes to add a Chris Isaak-styled wailing guitar part that Eva would certainly have loved. The tempo of the song is perfect – any slower and it would have been in danger of becoming boring.

Like *The Other Side*, the new album *Eva By Heart* was released by Brown's label Liaison Records a year after Eva's death. Joel E. Siegel, the music critic and professor of English and film studies at Georgetown University, wrote the liner notes. This was a real honour since Siegel had won the 1993 Grammy Award for Best Album Notes for his work on a Billie Holiday box set. He wrote: "Eva Cassidy was attracted to songs that express profound themes (love, loss, transcendence, redemption) drawn from a diversity of musical traditions which she transforms into haunting personal statements. Words are inadequate to capture the crystalline splendour of her singing, her pinpoint intonation and effortless control, her luxuriant multi-tracked choral backgrounds, her astonishing dynamics that range from the opalescent caress of ballads to full-throated, roof-raising blues and gospel shouts. The wonder of her sound is complemented by her fluent skills as an instrumentalist, guitar and keyboards, and the resourcefulness of her arrangements, which enfold her voice and guitar in layered harmonic textures. But even more impressive than her musicianship is the sheer, heartfelt emotion she conveys, cutting to the core of feelings all of us experience but can only stumblingly articulate."

Eva By Heart had already been released through Chuck's label, but Bruce Lundvall and Blue Note approached Eva's parents to express their interest in the possible release of other material. As a result Chris Biondo decided to give the Cassidys all the master tapes he'd made with Eva since 1988. He wanted to be sure he had done everything he could to secure a breakthrough for the "best singer in the world". Hugh paid Chris Biondo a reasonable sum for the tapes and Chris gladly accepted the offer.

After years of performing, singer Grace Griffith finally signed a contract with a small record company called Blix Street Records just before Eva's death. The Los Angeles-based indie label had tasted success with Irish singer Mary Black, who'd had a modest hit with 'No Frontiers', not to be confused with *No Boundaries*, the album that Eva recorded with David Lourim and Tony Taylor.

Grace hesitated to tell Blix Street managing director Bill Straw about her talented friend. She admitted in an interview that she was afraid that Eva would overshadow her, but she eventually decided not to hold back any longer. Grace copied a tape of *Live At Blues Alley*, making 'Fields Of Gold' the opening track, and sent it to Los Angeles. Bill Straw was immediately entranced, convinced that people would love it. At the same time he realised the tragic nature of this discovery: that Eva would become famous, but she would not live to see it.

Not long after hearing the tape Bill Straw was visited by his old British friend Martin Jennings, then managing director of Hot Records, an independent company based in the West Sussex village of Angmering. Hot Records was launched in 1984 from the backroom of an Australian record store called Didgeridoo in Darlington, near Sydney, where it began by distributing UK labels down under, before developing into the highly regarded label home of local heroes Ed Kuepper, The Triffids and The Celibate Rifles. English-born Jennings divided his time between Australia and the UK for some 20 years before starting the British arm of Hot Records in 1984 on the back of The Triffids' European success. After UK distribution deals with Rough Trade, Revolver, and then Vital, Jennings decided to make Hot Records its own distributor. At the time he first heard of Eva, there were three people working from a cottage in Angmering.

Wrote Tom Horan in *The Daily Telegraph*: "Hot Records is the company whose softly-softly success over the past nineteen years has seen it grow from a one-man-in-his-front-room operation to one of the most respected independent set-ups in British music."

Despite its small size, Hot Records handles over 2,500 titles, in every musical genre, and crucially had its own distribution arm. Bill played Martin the tape and before the first notes were through he exclaimed: "Who the hell is that?" Jennings was even more excited than Bill, further indication that European listeners would be particularly responsive to Eva's voice.

Determined to release an Eva Cassidy album, Bill Straw asked Grace Griffith to arrange a meeting with Eva's parents in April 1997. Over dinner, Hugh and Barbara quickly made clear their deep desire for the world to hear Eva's music. On November 2, exactly a year after Eva died, Straw and the Cassidys agreed that Blix Street would have the exclusive rights to release all recordings by Eva.

Because the Cassidys didn't have the necessary equipment in their home, Bill and Hugh visited Chris at his studio to listen to the demo tapes. After a few hours thought and discussion Bill decided to create an album that would combine highlights from the three previous Eva Cassidy albums released through Chuck Brown's Liaison Records. The album would be called *Songbird*. The only unreleased song on it would be a new version of 'Wayfaring Stranger'. Hugh advised Bill to use a stripped-down version, removing the Wurlitzer electric piano that Eva had liked so much in the mix, because he thought this version to be better, a feeling that is shared by other fans. The original version on *Eva By Heart* is steady and gets tired quickly, while on *Songbird* it is more restrained, the tension subtly building up to a real climax.

Martin Jennings of Hot Records agreed to release the completed *Songbird* album in the spring of 1998 in the UK, Australia and Asia, where he believed the chances of success would be higher than in the US. It was clear that Martin needed professional help to successfully promote the album and to this end he decided to approach one of the best record 'pluggers' in the business to bring it to the attention of the BBC's Radio 2, its natural home in the UK.

Tony Bramwell, born in 1941 in Liverpool, began his career in the music business as an assistant to The Beatles. Back in 1959 his old school friend George Harrison had just returned from Hamburg with bandmates John Lennon and Paul McCartney. Tony decided he would go to a Beatles gig in their hometown and offered to carry Harrison's guitar to get in for free. This auspicious start led to him becoming an aide to Beatles manager Brian Epstein, and a long-standing associate of the group. After The Beatles split, Bramwell joined Polydor Records as a record promoter, and he went on to receive an MTV award for his pioneering work on early pop videos. Following a period as a freelance record plugger Bramwell became disillusioned with a pop industry that had taken to prioritising looks and image over talent and took early retirement.

Martin knew Tony as a colleague from Warner Bros, when Tony had done promotional work for the company in the seventies, and he was willing to listen to *Songbird*. Tony loved the album, admitting that Eva's versions of the songs he liked were in most cases better than the originals. Tony needed a day to let everything sink in and to listen to the album again before he agreed to help. But after a second listen, his decision was made and his retirement was over.

The two men agreed to meet the following day, Martin bringing a box filled with copies of the album which he took to the BBC Radio 2 studios to distribute to everyone that mattered. At first many thought the music would be too old fashioned. It wouldn't be enough to get the voice of this unknown singer out there: Martin needed to write to as many influential music industry totems as he could.

Precise details of exactly when an Eva Cassidy song was first played on British radio – and by whom – has been a matter of conjecture among fans for some time, with both Mike Harding and Paul Jones in the running, though everyone defers to veteran DJ Terry Wogan as the man responsible for her ultimate success.

Harding, who as well as being a DJ is a musician and singer in his own right, heard his schoolteacher daughter's copy of *Live At Blues Alley* when he visited her at her home in Washington, D.C. in early 1998. Smitten by Eva's voice, he immediately went out and bought a copy for himself, and when he returned to the UK he had a feeling that 'Fields Of Gold' would be a hit on his weekly radio show on BBC Radio 2. His gut feeling was right. After debuting the song on UK radio in July 1998 the show was flooded with emails, phone calls and even emotional letters. At the time Mike believed that he was the first to play Eva's music in the UK but, in fact, just a week earlier, Paul Jones, the former singer with Manfred Mann, now a DJ, had played 'Wade In The Water' on his weekly Radio 2 *Rhythm & Blues* show.

But neither Harding nor Jones would take issue with the inescapable fact that the huge response to Eva's music that occurred several months later was down to Terry Wogan's support for her. However, according to a playlist that Hot Records received for royalty purposes, the first song by Eva that Wogan played was not 'Over The Rainbow', as most would assume, but 'Autumn Leaves' during the last week of August 1998. This seems to have been overlooked by everyone involved after the subsequent success of 'Over The Rainbow', which he played for the first time the following week. Two days later Wogan also played 'Fields Of Gold'.

Paul Walters, a BBC radio and TV producer, is noted for his work on Wogan's BBC Radio 2 breakfast show *Wake Up To Wogan*. Terry Wogan nicknamed him Paulie Walters, and he is known to millions as Dr Wally Poultry. Paul was one of Bramwell's first ports of call: "Dear Paul, I know you are a busy man, but you should really pay attention to this particular record. Cheers, Tony."

Personal relationships are valuable, especially in the highly commercialised world of the record industry and radio. Paul Walters received dozens of albums a day from hopefuls desperate to make their debut on the airwaves. If Paul had only the *Songbird* album cover to go on – a rather unattractive brown design with an out–of–focus Polaroid photo of an unknown girl-next-door – he might never have listened to it. But Paul knew Tony Bramwell, and if he had given up retirement to promote this new artist then she was certainly worth a listen.

Paul emailed Tony, promising to listen to 'Over The Rainbow', the track he'd particularly pushed. Tony's response was quick and to the point: "No, I'd like you to listen to it this very moment." Paul could not put off such a request. He listened to the song and it was immediately obvious that Tony hadn't been exaggerating. "This is bloody brilliant," he replied. "We are going with it tomorrow!"

Terry Wogan also had complete trust in Tony and he played 'Over The Rainbow' on his show the next day. "This is one Paul brought this morning by a lady called Eva Cassidy. Hope you like it!" At that moment, of course, neither had any inkling that Eva had passed away two years earlier. Wogan was enchanted by Eva's voice and quickly scanned the liner notes while the song was playing. As it faded out, he said: "That was Eva Cassidy, who it seems is tragically no longer with us."

Listeners responded in droves, more than 100 sending emails within 10 minutes of the song being played. The BBC's phone lines were jammed and letters and faxes poured in over the next few days. 'Over The Rainbow' might have been an old song but Eva's version had given it a timelessness that had clearly hit a chord with the public.

Taken by the singer and the public's response Paul and Terry played other tracks from the album, including 'Songbird' and 'Fields Of Gold'. Other DJs followed suit, Michael Parkinson, Bob Harris and Steve Wright among them.

British newspapers now turned their attention to the album by this unknown singer. *The Times* was the first, on July 24, its popular music critic David Sinclair noting: "*Songbird* gives some indication of the extraordinary purity of her vocal tone and her unusual facility for performing in virtually any musical genre." *The Daily Telegraph* wasn't far behind, reviewing the album on August 8: "If *Songbird* is anything to go by, she could have become a singer of considerable note." In *The Sunday Times* a day later Clive Davis wrote: "Cassidy's story ended at Chapter One, but she had a compelling story to tell none the less."

Suddenly *Songbird* was in demand. Hot Records responded quickly, arranging a fully fledged British distribution network. Sales climbed steadily and by the end of 2000 the album had sold an astounding 100,000 copies.

In November 2000 Blix Street Records sent Tony Bramwell the videotape that Bryan McCulley had made of the band's live recording for *Live At Blues Alley*. Eva's performance of 'Over The Rainbow' that night was far from perfect, with problems in image and sound quality, but it was genuine and utterly endearing. Tony believed the footage could make *Songbird* an even bigger hit album, and sent the tape to *Top Of The Pops*. Not being in the market for unknown singers with a cold and five-year-old black-and-white home-made films, producer Mark Hagen thought it too much of a risk to broadcast. But this was the best footage of Eva singing live and Tony believed in it. He suggested they use the clip at the end of *Top Of The Pops* on December 13, 12 days before Christmas. That way, if people turned off they'd be doing so at the end of the programme.

But viewers didn't turn off; in fact quite the opposite. The audience loved the clip and in the coming weeks it was requested again and again. Tony Bramwell stated in several interviews that the audience had made the connection between the old song they had enjoyed so much on Wogan's radio show more than a year before and the Blues Alley clip. They were as moved by seeing Eva for the first time as they were by her beautiful voice and tragic story. They appreciated the purity of Eva's music, free of theatrics and heavy production.

From that moment on the press became fascinated by Eva's life story. Martin Jennings received phone calls from the BBC, ITN, all the top newspapers, GMTV and *Time Magazine*. A report on *Tonight With Trevor McDonald* was aired in March 2001 and that same week Eva Cassidy's

Songbird outsold Dido's massive hit record *No Angel*, becoming the UK's number one album.

Despite his many past successes, Tony Bramwell feels the breakthrough he achieved for Eva Cassidy stands out as his proudest moment. His only regret was that Hot Records was too small to cope with Eva's overnight success. With better marketing and manufacturing, sales of the album would have been much improved.

Nevertheless, Eva's success was soon repeated in other countries, including Denmark, Sweden, Germany, the Netherlands, Romania and Australia, but the US was still to be conquered.

Eileen White, Chris Biondo's girlfriend, was asked to design an illustrated booklet for a new Eva Cassidy album that would be called *Time After Time*. Hugh and Barbara gave Eileen an envelope of photographs, including the promotional images that had been shot under the direction of Eva's manager, Al Dale. Eileen decided to use Eva's face shots, just as she had wished.

She also used a Larry Melton Polaroid which showed Eva making the peace sign. She was able to incorporate several of Eva's paintings and drawings, including a watercolour of a mermaid who seemed also to be making the peace sign with her hand. Eileen added one of Eva's poems, 'Springtime', and a handwritten set list from an Eva Cassidy Band performance. The clock face, a perfect counterpart to the album's title, came from an oil painting made for Chris. Green, Eva's favourite colour, was used to overall effect. It was the perfect portrait of Eva: a sweet and gentle artist and lover of nature.

Time After Time was released in 2000, four years after Eva's death, and is a collection of songs that she had recorded alone and with other musicians. The opening tune, 'Kathy's Song', composed by Paul Simon, was a shortened demo version. Eva's voice is restrained, matched by her guitar solo, paradoxically adding even greater emotion to the performance.

Bill Withers' 'Ain't No Sunshine' was recorded live at Blues Alley and is a clever follow-up to the opening track because it continues to demonstrate Eva's talents as a solo artist and acoustic guitar player. Eva combines both blues and folk in her version and the band's minimal accompaniment adds colour to what is essentially a solo piece.

Wayne Carson Thompson's 'The Letter', a hit for The Box Tops in 1967, is taken from the same Blues Alley concert. Opening as a ballad, the tension builds up throughout, with Lenny Williams and Raice McLeod lending the performance extra drive. Keith Grimes contributes an excellent guitar solo, though halfway through his guitar chords make it a bit crowded.

'At Last', a song by one of Eva's heroes, Etta James, is a studio recording. Eva's voice is suitably bluesy while her simple guitar playing gives the song a folk edge.

Eva was recorded singing her version of Cyndi Lauper's hit single 'Time After Time' at the Maryland Inn in Annapolis. Although not on the album, Eva introduced the song by saying: "This is one of my favourite songs that Cyndi Lauper did." Many other musicians covered the track, including Miles Davis who recorded an instrumental version that brings out the quality of the melody. On her version, Eva sings and plays guitar while Chris adds a modest bass part, giving the performance a strong foundation. Eva stripped the song back, returning it to its core melody. In fact it is much better than Cyndi Lauper's version.

'Penny To My Name' is a Roger Henderson song. Henderson was a singer-songwriter from Washington, D.C. who wrote for Broadway musicals and performed in coffee houses, concert halls and clubs, and he recorded several albums with Chris Biondo as his producer. Eva recorded this version as a demo for Henderson, who played the guitar part himself. Dan Cassidy added a violin part and Chris plays bass. Eva was not a huge fan of country music but the few recordings she did make are excellent, proving that she really could sing anything. Eva also contributed backing vocals to Henderson's song 'After You've Gone'. Sadly, Roger Henderson died on July 29, 2011.

Eileen White had a soft spot for 'I Wandered By A Brookside' and she listened to the song as she worked on the cover design. She thought it would fit perfectly on the album and she and Chris easily convinced Bill Straw to include it. Dan Cassidy came across the song on an album by a group called Whippersnapper which featured Dave Swarbrick, former violinist with the influential English folk-rock band Fairport Convention. Dan was fond of the song and he wanted Eva to hear it and so he gave her a cassette. It's a plain version, but seemingly simple songs are often the most difficult to play convincingly and Eva pulls it off.

One of Eva's own favourites was Harlan Howard's 'I Wish I Was A Single Girl Again', which she'd learned from her father. Her bluesy guitar playing mixes finger-picking with a lazy strum, and the vocal comes straight from the heart.

'Easy Street Dream' was another song composed by Steven Digman, who had written 'Say Goodbye' for *Eva By Heart*. A session orchestra under the direction of Bill Straw join Eva on the track, while Michael Finnigan's Hammond B-3 gives the song its bluesy character. Eva's high notes at the end of the tune would work well in front of a live audience, but on an album it sounds a bit over the top and distracts from the song's easy-going feel.

Steven Digman also wrote 'Anniversary Song'. For the album, Chris drafted in a group of Kennedy Center Opera House string musicians to play a new string quartet accompaniment composed by Lenny Williams, which replaced the original synthesiser. After the string ensemble had captured their parts they recorded extra layers. Lenny starts to play at the exact moment that Eva sings: "And the piano plays." Steven was very happy with the result; Chris' production is a real tribute to a singer who deserved to be complemented by the best possible music, and it moves to an impressive climax. This version was used in the 2001 film *The Man From Elysian Fields*, which featured Mick Jagger as Luther.

Eva recorded Joni Mitchell's 'Woodstock' live at the Maryland Inn on the same night as 'Time After Time'. The song became the anthem to a generation of hippies when Crosby, Stills, Nash & Young's version was used in the soundtrack to the documentary movie of the Woodstock Music & Arts Fair of 1969. Eva was too young to have experienced the hippie movement but she connected to everything it represented: a combination of freedom, humanism and the desire to make the world a better place. In 'Woodstock' Joni wrote "we are stardust", an image that is humbling but at the same time gives the listener an overwhelming feeling of being part of a magnificent universe, something that resonated with Eva.

'Way Beyond The Blue' was recorded in Larry Melton's bedroom and it is the oldest recording by Eva that has ever been released. The title had been 'Do Lord' when they made the rudimentary recording in the eighties. The basic idea for the song was fine: it showed the range of Eva's voice by allowing her to sing each of the parts in a gospel choir, accompanied only by handclapping. However, they were very young when they recorded it and Larry Melton, for one, was disappointed when he discovered this version on the album *Time After Time*. He had given the tape to Eva's family intending for it to be heard by them alone. To end an album that contains many surprising highlights with 'Way Beyond The Blue' was hardly a triumphal moment.

A year later, in 2001, Blix decided to reissue Eva's first solo album *Eva By Heart*. The album was first released on September 23, 1997, and had included a 12-page booklet with excellent photos of Eva. The local photographer who took the pictures had allowed Chris Biondo and his girlfriend, Eileen White, who had designed the packaging, to use the shots for free, since Liaison was not a huge record company and distribution was likely to be small. But after the success of *Songbird* in the UK the photographer wanted a fee for the use of the photos. Sadly, an agreement could not be reached and the booklet had to be redesigned with new photos and artwork.

It would not be the first dispute over money to darken the posthumous triumph of Eva Cassidy.

Chapter 13

No Boundaries

The year 2000 had seen Eva Cassidy finally become a star in a country she had never visited, her voice posthumously returned to its European roots. British record buyers, tired of a chart swamped with anonymous hip-hop stars and manufactured one-hit wonders, longed for beautiful songs that came from the heart. Eva's music was authentic; the real deal.

That was the positive angle on Eva Cassidy's posthumous success. The negative angle, as is so often the case in these situations, is the old axiom of 'where there's a hit there's a writ'. Regrettably this proved to be the case with Eva, and as the millions piled up in royalties so those who had an interest in this goldmine began to take sides, and simmering resentment was the result.

Initially, Hugh and Barbara paid Chris Biondo and the rest of The Eva Cassidy Band some money from the profits from album sales, with a cheque and a pleasant note coming to them every few months. However, in 2001, when *Songbird* became successful, the cheques and notes suddenly stopped. After Eva's sales took off, Hugh and Barbara were advised that they had no legal obligation to do so and Biondo's share of the income was reduced. When Chris enquired about shares for the other band members he was told he would have to split his own earnings with them. As the oldest band member, drummer Raice McLeod tried to get Hugh to change his mind with the result that he was no longer welcome in the Cassidy residence.

Chris shared his small percentage with Keith, Lenny and Raice but the members of The Eva Cassidy Band never met the Cassidys again. Chris had handed them Eva's tapes out of a desire for Eva's voice to be heard. "Without Chris there would have been no Eva Cassidy heritage at all," the other band members have pointed out.

In 1994 Bryan McCulley, the Blues Alley cameraman, had attempted to record footage of Eva's intimate performances at Pearl's in Annapolis. Eva sang as if she was performing to a small group of friends. Bryan plugged directly into the mixing console and he managed to produce a reasonable audio recording. One of the best songs that night was 'American Tune'. Eva listened to the tape as she worked on her murals in the school canteens and it was duplicated and circulated among her friends after her death.

The video recording was less successful: it had failed on the first night, but the second night had seen the capture of some great material. Eva never saw Bryan's videotapes, since she didn't like to look at herself.

The audio from this night eventually ended up on a bootleg album called *Live At Pearl's*, which was uploaded to the Yahoo Eva Cassidy Group in MP3 format by a mystery person in 2004. In June 2004, the family complained to moderator Scott Peterkin of Stone Mountain, Georgia, about possible breaches of copyright and demanded that the material be removed.

In an attempt to reduce the damage Blix Street pulled together the best parts of the Pearl's concerts, polishing them up for commercial release. They paid Bryan McCulley for the rights, but when they listened to the tapes they discovered that a clarinet had spoiled many of the songs – it would be practically impossible to remove the part, rendering them useless. The best clarinet-free songs ended up on several of Eva's later albums.

As Eva's star rose higher and higher her friend and fellow musician David Lourim and his business companions Tony Taylor and Al Dale decided to release an album of previously unheard material. In the eighties David Lourim had recorded many songs with Eva on his 24-track recorder. These sessions found an official release in 2000 on the Renata label under the name *No Boundaries*. The only cover on the album is Carole King's 'Natural Woman'. The other tracks are all originals, including 'Emotional Step', 'The Waiting Is Over', 'You Are', 'Little Children', 'I've Got This Feeling,' 'When It's Too Late', and 'On The Inside'.

Blix Street Records reacted furiously: *"No Boundaries* was released without the approval, blessing or support of the Cassidys, despite the misleading implication on the liner notes." Eva's parents had an exclusive contract with Blix Street Records which gave them approval rights over everything Blix Street released. Bill Straw advised The Cassidys to sue David Lourim.

Blix Street disputed that *No Boundaries*, a collection of old recordings, was a reflection of Eva's own musical inclinations, let alone her mature talent. At the very least the recording dates should have been indicated on the liner notes because without them it was misleading. Maggie Haven, Eva's former employer at Haven Art Studios, wrote on an Eva internet forum: "Many singers agree to sing on demo recordings of new artists' music when they are young and hungry. Eva recorded some rap music once too, and while she enjoyed the artists and the experience, the style did not reflect her own musical taste. The writer's original promotional recordings apparently did not catch on, and now that Eva's music is popular the tunes have been reworked and released to appear as a full-blown Eva Cassidy CD without her permission and despite the protest of those who represent her interests. I think this does her an injustice. I feel it misrepresents the mature Eva, and I believe that Eva would not have wanted this CD released as it stands."

Reactions to *No Boundaries* differed hugely. David Lourim reacted on the forum: "Many of the people who knew of these recordings thought they should be made available and that people would enjoy them. One example: reference the interview with Chris Biondo on this site and you will see he mentions 'Emotional Step'. Tapes were sent to some of the Eva fans found on this site to ask for opinions. They all agreed that this was something that should be released. There is a misconception that these are old songs. I have two problems with that. First is that you imply that Eva's ability was inferior when she was younger, which I can assure you was not the case. Second is that the songs are not that old. Most were recorded around the time she was recording *The Other Side*. She recorded 'Little Children' the same week as she recorded 'God Bless The Child'. I got to play on 'God Bless The Child' because the session got started after ours and I was asked to sit in by Chris, as was Jim Campbell our drummer. 'Way Beyond The Blue' is even older than anything on *No Boundaries*."

Eventually a settlement was reached in which the parties agreed that no further copies of *No Boundaries* were to be made, but those already produced could be sold.

Henrik Thiil Nielsen, creator of the Danish website EvaSongs and one of Eva's greatest fans, commented: "In some quarters, this album has been unfairly criticised and dismissed as being an unofficial release and therefore not a part of the Eva canon. This is a fine stand–alone album and obviously something that Eva willingly participated in. Sure, the music is not in the style with which we associate Eva, but nonetheless, it's still a fine album in its own right and is as important to the Eva Cassidy musical legacy as the early Quarrymen recordings are to The Beatles and the early Steel Mill recordings are to Bruce Springsteen. Therefore historically, as with the *Method Actor* album, they should not be overlooked. The other musicians on this album are Brian Lanier, Ira Mayfield, Bob Fiester and Jim Campbell. It's worth noting that the tracks 'The Waiting Is Over' and 'Little Children' are the same ones as featured on *Method Actor*. Al Dale, Eva's former manager, is credited as an executive producer."

Compared with official Eva album releases the arrangements on *No Boundaries* are far from original and the quality of the songs is poor. Eva deserves better, and it is certain that she wouldn't have liked the album – but for completist fans it is a must. It's up to the listener to decide whether music is good or not.

David Lourim also decided to re-release the *Method Actor* album with several bonus tracks. Blix Street Records asked David to retain the original album cover design, which he did, adding Eva's name in large letters. Eva's parents decided to sue David but Eva's loyal friend Ned Judy refused to cooperate in the suit. Ned reacted: "David Lourim produced an album named *Method Actor*. Eva sang lead and backing vocals while I played keyboard and arranged horn parts. Several other Bowie musicians participated as well. Eva and I both worked with Chris Biondo through these sessions because Chris was the engineer and owner of the studio where we recorded. Eva participated in *Method Actor* of her own free will. She chose to sing on it, and she was openly excited to be working on her very first album, on vinyl, a real album. She had often expressed a desire in creating an album cover which she did for *Method Actor*. This most probably was not her favourite kind of music, but it is what Eva chose to do at the time. She had sung with numerous hard-rock bands as a teenager, so she had much experience with this type of music and some of the players.

"Eva and I both gained experience from these sessions as we did from all of our recording experiences, and she undoubtedly relied to some extent on their experiences when producing her own recordings years later, as I often have throughout my musical career. I moved to California in 1988, just before *Method Actor* was pressed but I received a copy of the album, and several posters of Eva's amazing album cover.

"Dave Lourim was a longtime friend of Eva's and an integral part of her early career. He introduced her to me, and it was with me that Eva signed her first contract, establishing her first professional band Easy Street. Dave also introduced Eva to Chris Biondo, whose influence on her career is widely known.

"Dave Lourim should not be inhibited from selling his recording in which Eva Cassidy participated of her own free will. I understand that Eva, or her estate, should be entitled to some compensation for her work as featured sideman on *Method Actor* particularly in the light of her recent fame, without which this album would garner little demand or attention.

"I am concerned however, that someone other than Eva is trying to decide with whom Eva's voice should or should not be heard. And I am deeply troubled by news of a desire to outright destroy a product on which Eva worked so hard, eliminating a part of her career that doesn't fit nicely into someone's marketing plan. This is the very marketing logic that closed all doors to Eva while she was alive, a logic that would not allow her rich musical diversity. Eva transcended categorisation."

Part of the problem seemed to lie in the fact that David Lourim had released an album of "old, immature" material from the Method Actor period, and that potential buyers might be under the impression that it was a solo recording by Eva.

An important question in the debate was just how amateurish these recordings were. The group was short-lived but it was far more than a mere garage band. They had performed in public and had recorded and published a decent album. *Method Actor* had been produced at a professional recording studio during a number of sessions that were presided over by Lourim. He had played guitar, and the songs on the album were his own compositions. *Method Actor* was reviewed by the *Washington Post* and copies of the album had been distributed through several record stores.

Lourim hadn't had commercial success with any other records and he had been forced to abandon his songwriting for a career in business. In 2002 he signed a contract with Q&W Music and IDN to reissue the album with the amended artwork. The release of 45,000 copies was planned for June of the same year.

However, on June 24, 2002, the Cassidys and Blix Street Records made a legal claim alleging that Lourim had no right to re-release the album, focusing particularly on the fact that it might be confused with an Eva Cassidy solo project. They alleged that Lourim had violated copyright and trademark law and called for an injunction to stop distribution of the album *Method Actor*.

The first hearing was held on September 10, 2002. The Cassidys and Lourim testified, as did former members of Method Actor, and representatives of Blix Street Records, Q&W Music and IDN. What resulted was a denial of the injunction to prevent the album being distributed. *Method Actor* was a joint work and federal copyright law states that the authors of a joint work are co-owners of copyright, essentially giving them the rights to do with it what they please.

Further reinforcing this, there was also a written agreement that authorised Lourim to license and distribute *Method Actor*, albeit a short contract between friends. Created by Lourim himself and signed by Eva and several other group members, it stated that Lourim "had the right to use Eva Cassidy's recorded performances, financed by Lourim, in any form that Lourim may choose". The contract also made it clear that Lourim was to share any profits with Eva and the group's other members. Neither Eva Cassidy nor her estate had tried to terminate the agreement at any time, but it didn't really matter: the fact was that *Method Actor* was a joint work and as such Lourim maintained the rights to the material and its distribution.

At the hearing Blix Street alleged that *Method Actor* was "amateurish in comparison to the mature performances" that had helped Eva to find fame and further alleging it would "impair the singer's reputation". But *Method Actor* was not being passed off as an Eva Cassidy solo album, so the work simply didn't fall into this category. The court did rule, however, that stickers should be added to all unsold stock to more explicitly indicate that it was not an Eva Cassidy solo effort.

Despite an agreement being just around the corner, the case had to be reopened because of the inability of the Cassidys and Blix Street Records to agree on terms. The Cassidys were happy to give Lourim their blessing to distribute *Method Actor*, but the record company was apparently not.

As the case evolved, the Cassidys in fact decided to cooperate with their former opponent David Lourim, who had approached a producer regarding the use of the music of *Method Actor* in a film about Eva. Blix Street Records once again asserted their exclusive rights over all of Eva's works, but eventually the court found that the two parties were really working towards the same end and the case was dropped.

Nevertheless, the relationship between the Cassidys and Blix Street seems fraught with conflict. Sometimes they need each other and at other times they fight.

On March 27, 2004, *Billboard* magazine reported that Blix Street Records was suing Hugh and Barbara in another, unrelated case. Eva's parents had given filmmaker Allen Gelbard the green light to make a documentary feature on Eva. Hugh and Barbara had previously asked filmmaker Ken Burns, a documentarian who had made several films about the history of jazz and blues, to come on board but he had turned down the offer.

In the suit filed in the California Superior Court in Los Angeles, Blix Street Records alleged that the Cassidys' 1997 agreement with the label "gave the label exclusive rights to release all recordings by their daughter". The label hadn't granted synchronisation licenses for the proposed film soundtrack, but Blix Street alleged that the Cassidys had gone ahead with plans for the film despite this. In the end the litigation was dropped and plans for the film were shelved.

Henrik Thiil Nielsen, author of the website EvaSongs, reacted on the Eva forum on Yahoo: "We can only hope that these unsavoury lawsuits will inspire more people to check out Eva's music. If so, this will be the only beneficial effect they will have."

The lawsuits continued to fly around. Al Dale, who had put a lot of time and effort into trying to make Eva a star, had accepted the fact that success had not materialised. But when Eva suddenly achieved unlikely posthumous fame he called for his unpaid commission and expenses to be paid out of the huge royalties that Eva's work was now accruing. When the Cassidys didn't pay him Al immediately filed. Eventually Hugh was advised to pay Al what was owed, which he did in an out-of-court settlement.

Since so many were seeking to benefit from Eva's music, in 2004 Bill Straw decided to release a disc of material from other Eva albums which was entitled *Wonderful World*. Suggestions that Hugh and Barbara heard about the record only after it had been released remain unconfirmed, but Eva had wanted her music to be heard and to this end it served its purpose admirably. Regrettably, it had taken her death to see that happen. Sadly, with her success had come arguments, legal wranglings and much hurt, something that Eva would certainly have despaired of.

Chapter 14

Imagine & American Tune

An Eva Cassidy album entitled *Imagine* was released by Blix Street Records in August 2002. Its cover picture, taken by Walter Wunderlich, son of Barbara's cousin Dorothee, shows Eva standing atop a green hill near a village called Green Hill in Nova Scotia, a favourite holiday place for her and her mother. The drawing on the back cover of a little girl embracing a honeybee, reminiscent of Eva as a child, was her own artwork. She had originally designed it for a label on a honey jar. The black-and-white portrait on the interior of the album was taken by Larry Melton.

Imagine is a collection of unreleased studio recordings and live performances. The opening track 'It Doesn't Matter Anymore', taped at Pearl's in Annapolis in 1994, is one of the best, if not the best, song on the album. Written by Paul Anka but first popularised in 1959 by Buddy Holly immediately after his death in a plane crash, Eva's version resembles the cover by Linda Ronstadt, who was a major influence on Eva's singing. Whereas Ronstadt had been in a professional studio with the best equipment and the best musicians, Eva was performing to an audience more interested in their dinner. In short, this performance was not intended for an album but Eva's version grabs you immediately, especially the phrase "there's no use in crying", a perfect example of bittersweet comfort.

The version of 'Fever' on this album differs from the version on 1992's *The Other Side*. Dan Cassidy plays fiddle and, in fact, he recorded another version for his own less successful 1997 album *Dan Cassidy On The Fiddle*. Although the song is played in a swing tempo, it doesn't really "swing" and the drums are far from convincing. It is a disappointment after the strength of the opening track.

Sandy Denny was an English folk singer and songwriter who sang with the era-defining folk-rock band Fairport Convention before leaving to pursue other group and solo projects. Despite her talent (along with much critical acclaim, she is the only outside vocalist to have appeared on a Led Zeppelin record), mass commercial success eluded her and she suffered deeply from stage fright, low self-esteem and a lack of confidence. After a period of substance abuse and erratic behaviour, Denny died aged 31 in 1978 after falling down a flight of stairs, which induced a brain haemorrhage. The Cassidys credit her as a major influence on Eva, and for some time they attributed the mystery woman's voice in the commercial they'd loved as children to Sandy, but this has never been confirmed.

Eva recorded Sandy's most famous song, 'Who Knows Where The Time Goes?', at the Maryland Inn in the winter of 1995, on the same night as 'Time After Time' and 'Woodstock', all of which appeared on the *Time After Time* album (2000). It was the first time violin player Bruno Nasta had played with The Eva Cassidy Band. Years after this recording Chris Biondo discovered a Sandy Denny cassette tape under the seat of his car, Denny's name written in Eva's handwriting. 'Who Knows Where The Time Goes?' was one of the songs on it. Eva's singing is fine, but her guitar playing is a bit predictable.

'You've Changed' is a different version again from that which appears on 1992's *The Other Side*. It was a standard in Eva's solo repertoire, and it was also recorded at Blues Alley, but since it had already appeared on the duet album with Chuck Brown it was left off *Live At Blues Alley*. Lenny Williams' piano gives the recording its jazz feel and Eva can be heard coughing in the beginning.

Eva recorded her version of John Lennon's best-known post-Beatles song in Chris Biondo's studio very early on in their relationship. At that point she was a regular performer and in two days she recorded 12 songs. They were short versions because she wanted to show what she was capable of. Along with 'Imagine' she recorded 'Tennessee Waltz', 'Wade In The Water', 'Kathy's Song', 'Songbird' and 'A Bold Young Farmer'. Eva certainly doesn't top John Lennon's version, who sings it with more understatement, and somehow a piano seems more suitable than a guitar for accompaniment, probably because of Lennon's stately piano playing on his version.

'Still Not Ready', one of Eva's darker songs, was the only unknown song on this album, written by Chris Izzi and Leo LaSota. Chris Izzi, who combines musical leadership in two Baptist churches with playing in his band Izzi Does It, grew up in Bowie. He was a few years older than Eva but he was friends with "the Bowie kids" Larry Melton, Ned Judy and Mark Merella. Larry Melton had been bass player in Chris' band Fat Fingers and they had once shared a house, which is where Chris met Eva. In 1987 Fat Fingers recorded a couple of new compositions with producer Jeff Corbet. One of the songs they did was 'Don't Cry', which later became 'Still Not Ready'.

Years later Chris Izzi had a session with Eva's father Hugh Cassidy, with whom he played regularly. After they played 'Still Not Ready' Hugh said that he liked the song and that it sounded like a real standard. "Did you know that I recorded this song with your daughter years ago?" he asked Hugh. He then played Hugh the 1987 tape, who asked him to send it to Bill Straw.

Izzi was proud to make an appearance on *Imagine*, but it was double-edged: Bill had edited the song, removing both the sax intro and Chris Izzi's piano solo. Despite this, 'Still Not Ready' is one of the very rare modern-sounding jazz songs that Eva recorded, so it should be treasured.

Eva often performed Gordon Lightfoot's 'Early Morning Rain' as a solo. The version that appears on *Imagine* was also recorded at Pearl's. The combination of Eva's exceptional guitar picking and her restrained voice shows her at her best.

Covered by numerous artists over the years, 'Tennessee Waltz' dates from 1946 and was a hit for Patti Page four years later. Eva's version was recorded at the same time as 'Imagine' and although she wasn't keen on country music she admired singers like Emmylou Harris and sometimes found it hard to resist the lure of sentimental songs designed to send a shiver down the spine.

'I Can Only Be Me' is a Stevie Wonder number that appeared on the soundtrack to *School Daze*, a movie written and directed by one of Eva's favourite filmmakers, Spike Lee. The track that appears here is one of Eva's earliest recordings and is in fact the first with Lenny Williams on piano. Kent Wood took care of the strings. Lenny and Eva were huge Stevie Wonder fans and he remembers her knowing every one of his songs, including some more obscure tracks. Eva recorded two Stevie Wonder songs in her life, the other a funky version of 'Superstition'. In the liner notes Bill Straw writes: "If one of Eva's life ambitions was to be a backup singer for Stevie Wonder, perhaps her dream will finally be fulfilled in reverse, if Stevie Wonder sings along with Eva's version of his song."

The final song on *Imagine* is 'Danny Boy', written by Frederic Weatherly in 1919. 'Danny Boy', a popular Irish ballad often sung at funerals, with lyrics interpreted as a message from a parent to a son going off to war or at least leaving the Emerald Isle for far-flung places. Here, they seem a tribute to Eva's brother, living over the ocean in Iceland. After Terry Wogan, himself an Irishman, played Eva's version on his morning show he concluded by saying: "If that doesn't turn you to jelly, nothing will."

Eva was clearly fascinated by death and she was also affected by the changing of the seasons, the following lines being particularly noteworthy:

The summer's gone and all the flowers dying,
'Tis you 'tis you must go and I must bide
But come ye back when summer's in the meadow
Or when the valley's hushed and white with snow

The reviews for *Imagine* were similar across the board, first impressions being along the lines of: "What will be the next release? Eva Cassidy's voicemail messages?" as critic Mark Walker wrote on Amazon.co.uk. But when they took the trouble to listen the reaction was one of surprise. On

August 16, 2002 *The Independent* reviewed the album: "It's the folksier performances, such as Sandy Denny's 'Who Knows Where the Time Goes?', and her soulful solo treatment of standards such as 'Imagine' and 'It Doesn't Matter Any More' that reveal Cassidy's natural warmth: her gentle blues inflections on the latter bestow a pained resignation, while her impassioned simplicity even de-saccharinises 'Tennessee Waltz'."

Blix's next Eva Cassidy release was *American Tune* in 2003. It knocked Robbie Williams' *Live Summer 2003* off the UK album chart top spot, remaining there for two weeks. Of the tracks on the album, 'The Water Is Wide' and 'American Tune' were taped at Pearl's restaurant in Annapolis, 'It Don't Mean A Thing' at the King of France Tavern, part of the Maryland Inn, in Annapolis, and several others were recorded in Chris Biondo's studio. Some of the recordings came from guitar player Keith Grimes who made tapes of almost every song on which he played, including sessions and rehearsals with The Eva Cassidy Band and duets with Eva. After Eva's death he put the tapes in a box in his basement then hesitantly offered them for the album, fearing they would not be strong enough to be included.

Most of the material was certainly unusable. Several of the songs were recorded on Keith's Superscope and the vocal quality was terrible. Others were captured on Digital Audio Tape (DAT) and then copied onto cassettes, meaning they could not be remixed.

In 2002, a year before the release of *American Tune*, Chris Biondo sold the house in Upper Marlboro in which he had lived with Eva. While they were packing up Eileen White discovered several mementoes of Eva, including used tubes of paint and sketchbooks. But the most interesting find was five undeveloped rolls of film, of which Chris was unaware. Eileen decided to get them developed and discovered they contained Chris and Eva's holiday photos. She recognised the Moravian Church on the Virgin Islands that Eva had painted when she returned to the States.

Several photos from the films were used on the artwork for *American Tune*. In each of the images Eva is depicted connecting with the elements of nature: water, earth and air. The cover image shows Eva leaning against a fence, hat in hand, looking out over a green pasture.

The composition is relaxed and painterly, suggesting Eva had set it up herself, and there are other images on the missing film that echo this theme, including one with Chris lying in the grass wearing one of Eva's beaded necklaces. The colours in the film had distorted and faded, probably the result of accidental exposure, but this served to make the photos more interesting, reinforcing the soft painterly feel, so Eileen chose not to correct them.

Eileen also used several drawings in one of the sketchbooks they found. One shows a figure looking contemplative, with a thought bubble and arms outstretched, flying through the air. The image echoes the lyrics "And I dreamed I was flying" in Paul Simon's song 'American Tune'. A second sketch shows a small figure sitting on the back of a flying bird, which was printed onto the disc itself. Eileen brought all of the elements together with a dusty pink colour on the interior of the insert, all the better to reflect the soft tone in Eva's photographs and tie in with the lettering on the cover. Eileen's design was used for the US edition of the album, while in the UK Hot Records used a simpler version.

'Drowning In The Sea Of Love' is a robust rhythm and blues song, akin to the performances on *Live At Blues Alley* but seldom heard on Eva's other albums. Although Eva said she didn't like to sing loud songs, she sounds fantastic here and is still subtle in her approach. Lenny Williams plays a Hammond B-3 organ, and it is regrettable he didn't use this instrument more often with Eva. Keith Grimes' guitar solo is marvellous, though it was recorded slightly too loud.

'True Colors' was the second Cyndi Lauper song to appear on an Eva Cassidy album, after 'Time After Time'. Eva's arrangement of 'True Colors' was a favourite of both her's and the band and it had become a mainstay on their set list. The lyrics are once again resonant, a rainbow making another appearance.

'The Water Is Wide' appears here as a solo and was taped at Pearl's on the same night as 'It Doesn't Matter Anymore'. Hugh taught Eva the song, and she went on to sing it alongside Ruth and Celia in Mrs Walters' choir in junior high. In the version included here Eva slows the tempo down, giving it a more intense, focused feel than that of her tracks with the band.

'Hallelujah, I Love Him So', a studio recording, is a typical Ray Charles song in the sense that he often transformed gospel tunes into upbeat love songs. This studio version is shorter than the band's live version, which usually included an extra verse and an instrumental break. It misses the same level of enthusiasm it garnered in front of a real live audience, but it portrays Eva's light-hearted side, a characteristic not often heard on record.

The Billie Holiday song 'God Bless The Child' is taken from one of Keith Grimes' many rehearsal tapes (there is also a studio version on *The Other Side*). Jim Campbell plays drums on this version.

'Dark Eyed Molly', another studio taping, is a traditional song that Eva probably discovered from the repertoire of Fairport Convention, one of her favourite folk groups. She also recorded Joni Mitchell's 'Woodstock', inspired not by Crosby, Stills & Nash but by the version by Matthews' Southern Comfort, the group Iain Matthews formed after leaving the Fairports in early 1969.

The title song, 'American Tune', is the most appealing track on the album. Paul Simon recorded it for his *There Goes Rhymin' Simon* album in 1973 and *Rolling Stone* magazine in the US selected it as its song of the year. Simon has been criticised for stealing the melody from Johann Sebastian Bach's chorale 'St. Matthew Passion', but this was commonplace in the time that Bach composed the song and he in fact "borrowed" the melody from Hans Hassler's 16th century love song 'Mein Gmüth Is Mir Verwirret', and it was subsequently used in the famous hymn 'O Sacred Head, Now Wounded'. Eva learned 'American Tune', which was included in the family trio's repertoire, from her father and even when she was a child the combination of its haunting lyrics and the mesmerising melody, coupled with her startling voice, could move people. Bill Straw had three different recordings of the track and asked Grace Griffith to decide which one to use for the album.

'It Don't Mean A Thing', another taping from the Maryland Inn, features guest violinist Bruno Nasta, and was the first time the band played the song without a drummer. Nasta's violin part is clearly influenced by the famous French jazz violinist Stéphane Grappelli.

'Yesterday' – not just Paul McCartney's most famous song but the most covered track of any by The Beatles – was the only Beatles song that Eva recorded. Lenny Williams played it for the first time in his life during the recording session and Chris Biondo was unhappy with the noise coming from the pedals of Williams' Kawai baby grand. A few days later Dan added a violin part. Overall this is not an outstanding version of the song and Eva's gender-correct lyric change – "I'm not half the *girl* I used to be" – is unnecessarily distracting.

Eva and Chris had discussed the possibility of making a promotional video for 'You Take My Breath Away', the final track on *American Tune*. Eva didn't want to appear on the film, but the idea of paying tribute to the spiritual power of nature appealed to her and she came up with the idea of filming cloud formations with peeping sunbeams. Eva's friend, gifted singer-songwriter Niki Lee, tried to see this idea through some years later, with little success. The song's English composer, Claire Hamill, actually wrote it for her lover, who lived on the other side of the Atlantic. She was very surprised to discover that her song had ended up on an album that was successful in her own country.

In 2005 Amazon.com celebrated its 10th anniversary by naming its Top 25-selling CDs in the site's history. Eva Cassidy was number five, after only The Beatles, U2, Norah Jones and Diana Krall, but ahead of Bob Dylan (number nine), Bruce Springsteen (12) and Elvis Presley (25).

Chapter 15

Somewhere

No one expected there was sufficient unreleased Eva Cassidy material in the vaults for the release of another album but *Somewhere*, released by Blix Street in 2008, includes two new and surprising solo tracks, arguably the best solo performances Eva had ever given, 'A Bold Young Farmer' and 'Blue Eyes Crying In the Rain'.

The opening song, Eva's version of Dolly Parton's 'Coat Of Many Colors', came from Keith Grimes' collection of tapes and was recorded at Chris Biondo's studio in Glenn Dale in 1993. Eva accompanies herself, finger picking arpeggios on acoustic guitar, and Keith joins her on electric. Eva performed the song during her first solo gig, at a seafood restaurant in the Maryland town of Silver Spring. The lyric "Although we had no money, I was rich as I could be" seems to typify Eva's character.

'My Love Is Like A Red Red Rose', a traditional penned by Robert Burns, which Eva discovered on a radio programme about the Scottish poet, was recorded at the King of France tavern in the Maryland Inn during the winter of 1995.

'Ain't Doin' Too Bad', an upbeat R&B track, originally sung by American blues and soul singer Bobby 'Blue' Bland, was recorded at Blues Alley on the same night as the famous live album. Eva's voice was fine but the other band members weren't happy with the quality of their own playing. Keith, Raice, Lenny and Chris subsequently re-recorded their parts for the track on this album. Baritone and tenor saxophone player Leigh Pilzer wrote a big-band score that she played with her husband Chris on trumpet and trombonist Jen Krupa. The horns add power to the song. Audiences, the band and Eva loved the song but they never managed to record a solid version, so this version with additional instrumentation gives the listener a good idea of the band's capabilities. Lenny plays the piano as well as the Hammond B-3.

London producer Steve Lima provided a different take on Eva's version of 'Chain Of Fools'. Lima enlisted the services of sisters Leonie and Amba Tremain (of the British soul group Tremain) to add backing vocals during the summer of 2007. In 2001 Amba won first prize in the British television talent show *This Is My Moment* singing Eva's arrangement of 'Over The Rainbow'.

'Won't Be Long', the first song Aretha Franklin recorded for Columbia Records, is another rare happy Eva song. Sometimes referred to as 'When The Whistle Blows', it came from a rehearsal tape recorded in Chris Biondo's Glenn Dale studio in 1994, and features the highest note Eva ever sang in public. Raice McLeod plays country style on a stripped-down drum kit.

'Walkin' After Midnight' was recorded at the Wharf in Alexandria in 1993. The drummer on this Texas swing version of the Patsy Cline standard is JuJu House. The Eva Cassidy Band added this song to their repertoire for a performance on the second floor of country & western bar Cotton Eyed Joe's in Temple Hills, but they barely got an audience so they never returned. About three-quarters of the way through, the song takes a surprising jump into a higher octave but the sound quality is questionable.

Eva wrote and recorded 'Early One Morning' with Rob Cooper, a schoolfriend she met up with again years later, and they decided to write and record a song together. A combination of Appalachian vocal harmonies and lyrics fused to what was a traditional English folk ballad, it was recorded in Cooper's home studio in Calverton. Eva liked to experiment with many layers of vocals and this is a good example of her prowess in this area. Cooper plays dobro and electric lap-steel guitar on the track.

'A Bold Young Farmer', a traditional English folk song with a variety of different titles and slightly differing lyrics, was recorded in the Glenn Dale studio in 1995. A romantic tale of a maiden seduced, it is one of the best songs Eva ever recorded – if not *the* best – and she was absolutely right to introduce it to the band's repertoire. It is hard to imagine that anyone would not be moved by her version as she sings, "And on my heart put a snow white dove/ To let the world know that I died for love".

Dan Cassidy joins Eva's guitar with his fiddle in 'If I Give My Heart', recorded in Studio Stef in Kópavogur, Iceland, during Eva's visit there in 1994. Eva knew the song, written by John Pennell, from Alison Krauss' album *Rounder* (1987), and the Cassidys' version certainly brings the house down. Dan retains tapes of many of their duet recordings which remain unreleased to the public.

The Fred Rose country favourite 'Blue Eyes Crying In The Rain' was recorded at the Glenn Dale studio in 1995, and is the second highlight of the album. Eva's guitar playing is very effective, her voice restrained, and she manages to connect sadness with the notion of hope.

'Summertime' was another 1995 Glenn Dale recording. Eva sang this Gershwin standard with a gospel feel and adds simultaneous jazz chords and a walking bass on the lower guitar strings.

The album closer is 'Somewhere', initially known under the working title 'Hear'. Not to be confused with the *West Side Story* song that was memorably covered by Tom Waits, the lyrics for this were actually written by Eva – the only song she ever wrote that was recorded – and the music composed by Chris Biondo. Chris recorded the drum and synthesiser tracks and passed the tape to Eva to write a fitting lyric, and she attempted to put into words her confusion over how badly people can sometimes treat each other. They recorded the song several times and were quite happy with the chorus, but had trouble with the verses. It was typical for Eva to lose interest in a project if she wasn't satisfied with the end result. It was still unfinished when Eva died. Chris, however, remained excited about Eva's chorus.

After Eva's death Mike Schreibman of the Washington Area Music Association called Chris to ask if there was anything of Eva's that they could put on a WAMA sampler album called *DC CD 7 Washington Area Music Association (WAMA)*. 'Hear', better known as 'Somewhere', was the only piece of music that didn't fit stylistically with the rest of Eva's recordings, but it was thought that it might work on this sampler. Chris asked Mary Ann Redmond to rewrite the lyrics and melody for the verse and she also sang harmony on the chorus alongside Eva.

Chris' feelings were rather ambivalent when Bill Straw again asked him to work on the unfinished version of 'Somewhere' for the album of the same name. He did his best to make something of it but he was troubled by the fact that Eva would have hated to release sub-standard material. However, Hugh and Barbara liked the song and they gave Bill Straw permission to put it on the album, against Chris' will.

Although Eva helped Rob Cooper to write 'Early One Morning', 'Somewhere' is the only song she composed entirely by herself and is very different from all her other recordings. At the track's culmination we hear a complete orchestra with a pizzicato bass line and bagpipes paying tribute to an extraordinary singer.

The album *Somewhere* was released in August 2008 and was Eva's seventh posthumous album. Chris Biondo told a Swedish newspaper that he did not think Eva would have approved of the album: "She was a perfectionist and would no doubt have wanted to record new versions." However, despite Chris' concerns over the release of unpolished material, the album reached number four in the UK albums chart and was certified gold soon after. The public's appetite for new Eva Cassidy material was yet to abate.

Chapter 16

Michelle, Henrik and Laura

Three individuals in particular have played a key role in helping to promote Eva's music: Michelle Kwan, Henrik Thiil Nielsen and Laura Bligh. While Eva had become an acclaimed artist in Europe, where audiences took to her style of music quickly after her death, mass success still eluded her in her own country. However, that would change when in May 2001 ABC broadcast a brief but moving documentary on Eva in its late-night news programme *Nightline*. The effect was that over the following weekend all five of Eva's albums that had been released up to that point climbed to the top spots in Amazon.com's sales chart. The documentary has since become one of the most popular instalments of *Nightline* ever to have been aired.

Sales in the US were good, but still small compared with the UK. 'Fields Of Gold' had helped to make the compilation album *Songbird* a number one album in the UK. However, the song was to get a second burst of life, introducing Eva to a much wider audience.

The American figure skater Michelle Kwan chose Eva's version of 'Fields Of Gold' for a routine that she performed during several championships, including the 2002 Winter Olympics in Salt Lake City, Utah. Kwan's coach had discouraged her use of the song since it was unusual to skate to anything other than instrumental tracks, and he thought the lyrics would distract the audience or, worse still, the judges.

But Kwan was absolutely certain of her decision: she had never come across a song that relaxed her more while skating.

Kwan skated several times to 'Fields Of Gold' during the winter of 2001, and her love for the song was plain to see as she sang along to it during her routine. During the 2002 Winter Olympics Kwan wore a glittering Vera Wang costume while she performed the same routine in front of millions of viewers. She won bronze and Eva's version of the song was introduced to a new audience around the world.

In the spring and summer of 2003 Michelle Kwan toured the United States with Champions On Ice, a touring ice show featuring Olympic champions and other high-quality skating novelty acts. Hugh and Barbara saw the show in Baltimore and met Michelle Kwan backstage with Blix Street Records boss Bill Straw. He had an unexpected gift for Michelle; due to the publicity Kwan's performances generated for Eva's music, *Songbird* had been certified gold in the United States. Bill presented Michelle with a replica gold disc for her part in this success. Eight years after her death Eva had finally conquered her own country.

Henrik Thiil Nielsen, born in Copenhagen in 1960, had been a musician in the seventies and is a lifelong music fan. He first came across the name Eva Cassidy in a 2000 review of another female vocalist who was compared with the Maryland singer. His interest was piqued but he quickly discovered that Eva's albums, which were hits in the UK, were not widely available in his native Denmark. However, as soon as Henrik heard Eva's voice his fascination for the singer grew.

He communicated with other Eva fans via a Yahoo newsgroup where he made contact with Torbjörn Skobe, a Swedish fan. Together they decided to transcribe Eva's songs for guitar, Henrik's degree in English helping him to translate the lyrical content. Eventually they started the website EvaSongs, at evacassidy.dk.

Initially the site focused on transcribing every one of Eva's arrangements for guitar and voice. Now, ten years later Henrik can be described as a Professor of Eva. His love for the singer moved him to contact everyone she had known, and his website has become a fount of knowledge related to the late singer. He has discovered that some fans are obsessive to the point that Eva's music is virtually a religion for them. Henrik came to realise how popular he and his website had become when he received a call from Andrew Bowles, then managing director of Hot Records, asking for his opinion on the poor showing of sales of Eva's records in Denmark. Henrik replied that, in general, Danes have a rather frivolous attitude towards music, viewing it simply as entertainment and a way of having fun rather than something to be taken seriously. Consequently, the emotion that Eva put into her music didn't resonate with them as it had with the Brits. He also believed that the company that distributes Eva's albums in Denmark, MNW (Music Network), didn't see her music as being the spearhead of their enterprise.

Henrik continued to build up an enormous archive including photographs, digital newspaper clippings, reviews, rare albums and bootlegs. However, when he tried to share it with the visitors to his website he received a second phone call from Bowles with a friendly, but urgent, request to stop as his "disruptive activities" could harm record sales.

Despite these frustrations, the site continues to be hugely popular and Henrik and Torbjörn still translate almost everything that Eva appears in into Danish and other European languages.

In 1999, Laura Bligh, daughter of Hugh's older sister Isabel Cassidy, started a website dedicated to Eva called evacassidy.org. Twelve years later this extensive site has become the most important and interesting source of information on Eva Cassidy's music. In Laura's own words: "For some fans the pleasure of listening is enough. Others want to know more: 'Who was this remarkable singer? Why haven't we heard of her before? Are there more albums?' This web page can be your gateway."

Remarkably, 12 years after starting the website Laura still has plenty of current and relevant information to regularly refresh the 'What's New' page. Aside from logging every Eva Cassidy recording (including the bootlegs, which Laura asks fans to avoid), she publishes reviews of Eva's CDs and DVDs from all over the world, sometimes with the help of devoted fans such as Henrik, who translate them into English for her. She also posts radio and TV broadcasts containing interviews with people who worked with Eva.

Laura's website has a huge collection of published articles including older newspaper clippings that were later proved to be false, with Laura's help, including the following: "This is my 'pet peeve'. EVA DID HAVE HEALTH INSURANCE! When she left her job at Behnke's Nursery she joined the musicians union (D.C. Federation of Musicians, Local 161-710), and signed up for group medical insurance through the union. I feel it is important to mention this because it is one of the many excellent reasons for musicians without 'day jobs' with benefits to join their local unions. The issue of health insurance must seem odd to people outside the United States, but regrettably it is a Big Deal here."

Laura has talked with almost everyone who played a role in Eva's musical life. She has done interviews with Chris Biondo, Keith Grimes, David Christopher and Al Dale, along with those who have a fresh view on Eva's music, including Steven Digman, Grace Griffith, Eileen White and Eva's first superfan, Mike Dove. She discusses all of her songs, including their history and their meaning to Eva.

Surprisingly, Laura has published a self-penned screenplay about Eva's life on her website. It is yet to be picked up for production, so she shares it in full with Eva's fans.

The website includes many special features, including photographs, a biography, a Q&A section, a guest article by fan "Eric from Silver Spring", a fictionalised version of the night that *Live At Blues Alley* was recorded, entitled 'You Are There' and much more.

The most popular section of the site is the guestbook and in the unlikely event that you are missing any facts you can contact webmaster Laura Bligh herself, who is an excellent source of information on all things related to her late cousin.

The Cassidys regularly ask Laura to remove controversial content, which puts her in an awkward position: she is not in the habit of rewriting history but neither does she want to be looked upon as the family pariah. She needs to remain on good terms with everyone to see her self-appointed job through. However, the Method Actor page remains on her site as a symbol of Laura's journalistic independence – although the Cassidys would do anything to remove it.

Through both of these websites, Eva's story continues to live on for fans new and old to discover.

Chapter 17

Songbird, Her Story By Those Who Knew Her

British TV filmmakers Rob Burley and Jonathan Maitland became involved with the life story of Eva Cassidy in March 2001 when they were assigned to make a short film for ITV's *Tonight With Trevor McDonald*. They realised that there was more to the story than could be covered in one documentary alone so they decided to write a biography, which they called *Eva Cassidy: Songbird, Her Story By Those Who Knew Her*.

From the outset, Hugh and Barbara's lawyer assisted in arranging all interviews, with Eva's former housemate and promoter Jackie Fletcher also helping. The Cassidys also negotiated a share in the profits from the book. Burley and Maitland's job would have been impossible had they not agreed. Not only did they have little choice, but the work was completed in a hurry because no one knew how long Eva's fame would last.

Most of the interviews took place in the lawyer's house and every conversation was taped. Burley and Maitland's book contains only direct quotes linked by occasional facts. Some participants were displeased by the way in which they were portrayed, while those with contentious opinions or those who "knew too much" were simply ignored or edited. Drummer Raice McLeod was invited to tell his story, but for reasons that he still doesn't fully understand he was left out of the book. Eva's former manager, Al Dale, and David Christopher (formerly Lourim) also failed to make the cut. The biography had turned into something of a Disney-style fantasy.

Songbird was targeted at the UK market and though it sold well a number of readers felt that something was missing. Reading *Songbird* is like watching the first scene of a creepy movie: innocent children are playing on a beach and the sun is shining on a calm sea, but ominous bass notes create a sense of foreboding – something terrible is going to happen, yet you don't know what it is.

A year later the American version of the book was released, this time with the family lawyer Elana Rhodes Byrd credited as a co-author. In her preface to the book she writes that she "helped to organize the material and thoughts for Rob Burley's interviews". There was little attempt to hide the fact that the book was designed to promote a positive image of Eva, essentially little more than a PR exercise.

This was a mistake. Though *Songbird* was a bestseller for publisher Orion in the UK and a reasonable seller in the States, it threw the unfortunate Cassidy family into the eye of a media storm. They became ever more reclusive, shielding themselves from unwanted questions and confirming only as much as they wanted to. A side effect of this was that it inspired unsavoury rumours about the reality of Eva's life, certain passages leading to wild speculation on internet forums. Although Laura Bligh removes anything negative from her guestbook pages, it's not difficult to find harmful gossip cropping up elsewhere on the internet.

One of the criticisms of the book was that it lacked information about the German past of Eva's mother, Barbara. Her family name, Krätzer, did not appear in the book. Barbara's early life is summed up in just one sentence: "Barbara grew up into a childhood of hardship in Hitler's Germany in 1939, six weeks before the outbreak of war."

As it happened, Barbara's father had been a communist who resisted the Nazi regime for as long as he could. But why was this left out of

Songbird? Was the family afraid that the word "communist" would scare Americans?

Songbird paints a picture of children who tried desperately to remain on their father's good side: "When they played music together that's when Hugh enjoyed his children most." Hugh is also quoted in the book as regretting behaving like a hard taskmaster towards his daughter. Reading between the lines you get the impression that Eva and Hugh had found it difficult to communicate.

Magnus Eriksson, a distinguished Swedish critic, wrote in a review of *Songbird* that there was the suggestion in the book that Eva was plagued by inner conflicts, while Eva's friend David Lourim posted a reaction on an internet forum: "Eva did the solo acoustic shows for a few reasons, the biggest being it was easier to find gigs playing solo and the expectations were less. On *Time After Time* some of the songs are incomplete. This was because she recorded them as demos to help get gigs so they didn't have to be complete. Now these recordings are being used to shape Eva into a folk singer, something their attorney admitted in court at the preliminary injunction hearing. Eva would have been very unhappy about all this. The correct choice would have been to leave everything in Chris Biondo's control. You would have gotten a truer sense of the real Eva and there would be no Method Actor dispute. But Eva left no will. She didn't think what she had done was worth anything. So, why bother?"

The rumours didn't just attract visitors to internet forums. Because of Eva's fame, newspaper journalists started to dig around and where *Songbird* withheld information, the papers tried to fill in the gaps. The eternally salacious and now defunct *News Of The World* published a story about Eva's alleged "secret affair with a woman". This highly speculative and incorrect story no doubt stemmed from the fact that, regrettably, *Songbird* rather naively described a woman who broke off all intimate relationships with men and found a deep friendship with a woman to whom she said: "Let's be together, just the two of us." With a tabloid press obsessed with sex and a society open to celebrity tittle-tattle, it is easy to subscribe to the illusion that what is being described is a lesbian relationship. It was completely untrue.

For Eva's close friend Ned Judy the *Songbird* book and low level of journalism it provoked gave him reason enough to refuse all interviews regarding Eva.

Laura Bligh was also disappointed with the outcome of the book. "Brief casual mentions would have been preferable to an obvious omission that calls attention to itself," she points out.

Chapter 18

'Over The Rainbow' and Katie Melua

A musical about Eva's life, called *Over The Rainbow*, was staged in 2004. Author Brian Langtry noticed an advertisement in *Stage* magazine for the show *A Slice Of Saturday Night*, produced by Phoenix Productions, a company based in his hometown of Ashby-de-la-Zouch, a small market town in Leicestershire. Intrigued by the fact that a professional production company was so close by, he contacted them and discovered a mutual fascination with and appreciation for Eva's music. With the help of Phoenix he produced the show. The musical went on a preview tour from March to November in 2004. Loreto Murray played Eva and Gus MacGregor, who had been lead in the musical *Buddy*, took the role of Chris Biondo.

Producers Stephen Leatherland and Brian Langtry travelled to Washington, D.C. in 2005. With the help of Chris and his girlfriend, Eileen White, they explored places that had been important to Eva, which led to them incorporating photos and video clips from their trip into the musical.

Stephen and Brian enjoyed the company and hospitality of the members of Eva's band. They sought out clubs and venues where Eva performed, they strolled through Annapolis, spent time in Oxon Hill,

168

explored Bowie, visited Cedarville Forest, Behnke's Nursery, Old Alexandria and the Naval Club that had seen Eva's first performance, where she had knocked over the microphone. They met Eva's cousin Laura Bligh, spoke to Grace Griffith, who was recording a new album with Chris during their visit, and saw Mary Ann Redmond perform in a club in Bethesda. Both concluded that they couldn't understand why such a fabulous singer as Mary Ann Redmond wasn't a major star. But it wasn't hard to see why when hardly anyone in the area had the faintest notion of Eva's massive fame in Europe.

During 2004 Phoenix Productions contacted the Cassidy family, forwarding them a script and including a letter in which they queried a number of issues, all of which were resolved in the belief that they would share in the profits. On their visit to Robert Goddard School Langtry and Leatherland asked a member of staff, who had known Eva, whether it would be possible to meet with Larry Melton and they left Langtry's phone number. When Larry was contacted he presumably alerted the Cassidy attorney to the producers' presence in D.C. She immediately called them, and asked them why they hadn't planned to visit the Cassidys. The answer was simple: because this same lawyer hadn't answered their email request to do so. Having spoken to Eva's former band members they knew what was behind this sudden turn of events: the Cassidys didn't want anyone else to earn a penny from Eva's name. This would mean giving the Cassidys a share of all future profits. Brian and Stephen decided not to talk to Hugh and Barbara or their lawyer and to go ahead with the show. Instead, the makers changed the songs and because the Cassidy family have laid claim to image rights, didn't use any photographs of Eva Cassidy in the promotional material. A painting was commissioned which has appeared on the poster ever since.

The inaugural premiere of the newly reworked *Over The Rainbow* show was held at the Theatre Royal, Margate and was attended by BBC producers who were about to go to Washington, D.C. to make a documentary about Eva. In the event, the BBC's production team returned from D.C. without having reached an agreement with the Cassidys' family lawyer regarding the scope and content of the proposed documentary.

The show itself has attracted large audiences. It is about to start its 11th tour of UK and has toured Ireland four times, appeared in Holland where it won the theatre 'Best Show of the Year Award' and been booked in to be the first British musical to appear in Dubai. Chris Biondo came to the UK to see the show during the 2005 tour at the Hayes Theatre in London and drummer Raice McLeod appeared as himself on February 2, 2008 – Eva's birthday. In the autumn of 2005, Brian Langtry compiled an eight-page document detailing and refuting the vague allegations of plagiarism referred to in a letter from the Cassidys' English legal representatives.

Over The Rainbow is built up from short scenes from Eva's life and interspersed with lots of music, starting with the gospel song 'How Can I Keep From Singing?'. Many of the actors play instruments themselves, which has led to the portrayal of Eva's sister Margret playing the violin instead of brother Dan. The best section of the musical revolves around the famous 1996 live concert at Blues Alley. Many fans see it as their only chance to get an impression of what an Eva Cassidy performance would look and sound like.

At the beginning of the theatre season 2010/2011 actress Zoe Tyler was drafted in to take over the lead role. She appeared on the morning show *BBC Breakfast* and sang a pleasing version of 'Fields Of Gold'. When she was asked what Eva Cassidy's parents and other relatives thought about the play, Tyler hesitated for a moment and then replied: "Oh, they love it. As a matter of fact, this is our sixth season. Everyone loves it! Someone told me: 'I had to cry all the time, but I will come again tomorrow!'"

In reality no one from the Cassidy family has ever seen this musical.

It was when Eva saw and heard Buffy Sainte-Marie that she decided she wanted to be a singer. Later, other singers would follow in Eva's footsteps. Georgian-Irish-British singer Katie Melua cites Eva as an inspiration. Katie was a student of the Brit School, a performing arts school in London that had launched the careers of many pop singers and actors in the UK and beyond. Like many other young girls, Katie was a fan of The Spice Girls and hip-hop rappers, but the first time she heard Eva Cassidy sing 'Over The Rainbow' she was struck by the depth of Eva's simple delivery and unpretentious style. Eva showed Katie that music wasn't all about fashionable clothes, hi-energy dance routines and flashy make-up. She sounded old fashioned but fresh and new at the same time.

Katie was so overwhelmed with joy at her discovery of Eva that she composed a song about her, 'Faraway Voice', which appeared in 2003 on Katie's debut album, *Call Off The Search*, which went on to be a massive hit, launching the singer-songwriter to superstardom and world fame.

In 2004 Katie toured in the US, performing at The Birchmere in Washington where Eva had once played. She felt the presence of Eva, opening the concert with 'Faraway Voice' and encoring with Eva's 'Anniversary Song'. Katie knew that Eva was not as popular on home turf as she was in the UK so she told her audience that Eva's version of the song was spectacular and could be found on the *Time After Time* album, which everyone had to check out.

In 2004 a special edition of *Call Off The Search* was released with a bonus DVD called 'Onstage And Backstage', which included Katie's version of 'Anniversary Song'.

On Christmas Eve 2006 this modest singer-songwriter who had done so much to put Eva Cassidy's songs on the map sang 'Over The Rainbow' alongside footage of Eva on the BBC's *Duet Impossible*. A year later her and Eva's voices were cut together on 'Wonderful World', which was released to raise money for the British Red Cross and went to number one in the UK singles charts on December 16, 2007. Katie's management had sought permission from the Cassidy estate, which they had received, but it later transpired that Bill Straw had benefited from the duet's royalties, whereas Hugh and Barbara hadn't seen a single penny. It was the umpteenth example of the fraught relationship between Blix Street Records and the Cassidys.

On August 20, 2003 Swedish television planned to broadcast a Rolling Stones concert that was cancelled for legal reasons. In its place video clips of Eva Cassidy performing at Blues Alley were shown. As a result the broadcast attracted many viewers that would otherwise have missed it.

Other musicians continued to be inspired by Eva's music. In 2004 Michael Ingram, Eva's fellow band member from Characters Without Names, released a CD with songs from the soundtrack to a film called *Anywhere But Here*, which was directed and produced by Michael. Eva had a scene in the movie that was later scrapped. The CD includes the song 'Baggage', which is sung by Eva, but the album sold very little.

Also in 2004, Mary Chapin Carpenter recorded *Between Here And Gone*. One of the tracks on the album is 'My Heaven' and includes the line: "More memories than my heart can hold/ Eva's singing 'Fields Of Gold'".

Keter Betts, bass player on *The Other Side*, died in 2005 at the age of 77. On New Year's Eve that same year Kent Wood, who had played organ on 'Wade In The Water' and electric piano on 'Wayfaring Stranger', died in a car accident. Kent played the piano when Eva sang 'What A Wonderful World' for the last time in her life at The Bayou.

In October 2006 Paul Walters, the producer of Terry Wogan's morning radio show, sadly died. Wogan opened the show with 'Over The Rainbow', saying: "Well, it just had to be Eva who was first to be played this morning – would have been no other I guess."

In 2007 pianist and organist Hilton Felton died. He had worked with Chuck Brown and appears on several Eva Cassidy recordings including 'Oh, Had I A Golden Thread'.

Grace Griffith recorded her fifth album *My Life* in 2006, which Chris Biondo and Lenny Williams produced. In 1998 Griffith was diagnosed with Parkinson's Disease and she has her good and her bad days.

As for the regular members of The Eva Cassidy Band, Lenny Williams and Chris Biondo continue to work together and have won nine Emmy awards for their musical scores to several television documentaries. Lenny won a Teton Award for Best Original Score at the British Jackson Hole Wildlife Film Festival in 2007. Their work can be seen on a regular basis on the National Geographic channel. Lenny is also pianist of Capitol Steps, a popular political satire group. Raice McLeod and Keith Grimes still play together in The Mary Shaver Band.

Chapter 19

Hollywood, Eva's Artwork and *Simply Eva*

In the years since the death of his sister, Dan Cassidy and his family have received many heart-warming requests from would-be filmmakers who are keen to become involved in the production of a movie about Eva. Creative people are inspired by Eva – her life seems to fire their imagination. Dan has met some of the most enthusiastic filmmakers but no one has yet succeeded in their quest to make an Eva Cassidy biopic. Having written such a script herself, Eva's cousin, Laura Bligh, jokingly states: "My 15-year-old son is probably the only one who hasn't written a film script about Eva Cassidy."

American filmmakers Bob McCarty and Allen Gelbard were first to start work on a film. They conducted research and interviewed participants for more than a year, but the project ran aground when Bill Straw and Eva's parents couldn't come to an agreement regarding the use of Eva's music. Bob and Allen returned to Los Angeles, disappointed. The same happened to American film producer and author Brad Bredeweg.

But not every filmmaker intended to produce a controversy-free hagiography of Eva's story. Actress and film producer Meg Ryan promised to reveal "the dark side of the reclusive and unhappy singer", as she described Eva Cassidy in an interview with *The Times* on September 1, 2002. She wanted her film to balance the views of the *Songbird* biography. Ryan interviewed friends and people from the music industry who described Eva as a "temperamental and shy junk-food addict... and tormented by depression". Ryan explained all to an intrigued journalist: "There is a dark side to Eva which may offend the fans but will interest more people than a plaster saint." The interview upset devoted Eva fans, like Joanne Cooling, who reacted by expressing her displeasure at "anyone who screws around with Eva".

The effect of the failed attempts to make a feature film about Eva Cassidy's life was that Bill Straw decided he would make his own. In 2006, Straw met with Niki Lee, former wife of piano player Lenny Williams, and a singer, author and friend of Eva. Lee offered Straw a tape of a concert of The Eva Cassidy Band with Mick Fleetwood playing the drums but he wasn't interested because the audience in the drummer's club, Fleetwood's, made too much noise. Straw then told Lee about the failed attempts to make a film about Eva's life. Straw said he still wanted to make a film about Eva and Niki Lee promptly offered to write a script, which Straw encouraged. She thought long and hard about the best way to accurately reproduce Eva's life on the screen. She didn't want to make a Hollywood kitsch drama and concluded that an animated movie would be in the spirit of Eva. She decided to use one of Eva's own cartoon characters to play her, and that she would inhabit a world based entirely on Eva's artwork. The idea was reminiscent of the project that Eva and Chris had in mind for the video of 'You Take My Breath Away'. She showed Bill Straw the results, but they never came to fruition.

In 2007 Straw met with Amy Redford of AIR Productions, producer of the *Sex And The City* television series and various films, to discuss the proposal. Amy told Bill that she wasn't interested in an animated film but that she wanted to transfer Eva's life to a real Hollywood movie, which would attract larger audiences. Amy would ask her father, Robert Redford, to take the role of Hugh Cassidy and Kate Winslet or Nicole Kidman to perform the lead role.

A new scriptwriter, Kathryn Sheard, was drafted in and she has written the first script to receive approval from Hugh and Barbara. At the time of writing, this is an ongoing project.

In 2010 several British newspapers mentioned that Kate Winslet was in line to take on the role of 'songbird' Eva Cassidy. Bill Straw believes that the film will finally see the light of day in due course.

The most striking difference between Eva's music and her painting is that she had yet to find her own voice in her artwork. Maybe this was because much of her work was intended as gifts for family members or friends and she had the recipient in mind as she worked. Some of her art is clearly influenced by artists such as the surrealist Salvador Dali, while her painting *Cape John* resembles Van Gogh's famous *Starry Night* and *Night Flight* has the typically Van Gogh trees.

Fine artists often have to work their entire lives to find their voice. Sadly, Eva had no such opportunity. The energy she had left after a full day of work was usually spent perfecting her music. Her mentor Chris Biondo supported her musically, but Eva missed the equivalent for her visual work.

Despite the obstacles Eva had a natural ability to perceive the true essence of things she saw; she could observe something and see clearly into its heart, and reproduce this on canvas. Her technical skill enabled her to create atmosphere, which she achieved with clever use of colour and light.

Eva was a prolific artist and the bulk of the material has attracted interest largely because it was Eva the singer who created it. Nevertheless, there are a few pearls among the everyday material. *Night Flight* depicts a fish flying through the air and a boat on dry land. It is an intriguing composition with intelligent and original use of colour that gives it a supernatural feel. Eva liked to create conundrums, which is evident in the many mysterious bubbles in her work. The bubbles could very well be symbolic of Eva's own personality – her inner self, closed and vulnerable. Compare Salvador Dali's *Woman Bubbles*.

One small painting hints at the direction Eva may have taken had she had more time. It depicts an unknown young woman, and is the first to truly bear Eva's personal stamp. Appearing both suspicious and bored at the same time, the woman is clearly staring at something but we don't know what. The painting recalls old photographs that show a young Eva turning away from the photographer. Perhaps it was an early self-portrait. The canvas shows through in the background and Eva's use of dark and light in different shades of green clearly indicates a budding talent that never had a chance to fulfill itself.

Vincent van de Kerk is an independent museum advisor and fundraiser for Arte-Quattro, a Dutch art office, and, among other things, he manages and supervises art exhibitions. In 2010 he discovered that Eva Cassidy's art had never been displayed outside of album inserts. Van de Kerk decided he'd like to organise an exhibition that would showcase Eva's paintings, drawings and beaded necklaces in a national Dutch art museum. He asked several of Eva's closest friends and family, including Chris, Ruth and Celia Murphy and her parents what they thought of the idea. They all reacted positively, with Barbara even stating that it was her deepest wish that Eva's work should be shown in a real art museum.

When Vincent approached several people in the art world with his idea their reaction was discouraging: Eva's art was not modern or otherwise remarkable. But as a singer Eva had reached large audiences and those audiences would certainly be interested in an opportunity to see her art for the first time.

Vincent suggested that the ground floor of a large hospital in Amsterdam was the perfect venue to stage an Eva Cassidy art exhibition. This AMC gallery not only owns the largest collection of modern art in The Netherlands, receiving 12,000 visitors a day, but it would also be a nod to the Johns Hopkins Hospital in Baltimore, where Eva's room had been transformed into an art gallery. The exhibition would create greater interest in Eva's life, art and music.

When Vincent presented his proposal to the family he was asked about its potential for selling Eva's paintings, but sadly the whole idea ran aground when the family declined to become involved.

During the same period the National Gallery of Art in Washington also showed interest in Eva's art. It might have been a good idea to connect Eva's paintings to those that she was inspired by during her family visits to the same gallery.

So far, nothing has happened with Eva's artwork in the National Gallery of Art in Washington. Consequently, the world is yet to see an exhibition of Eva Cassidy's creations.

Simply Eva, an album of solo performances by Eva, was released in 2011. It is the first album to be given over entirely to Eva's solo interpretations of the songs she loved, accompanying herself on acoustic guitar, free of any further production or instrumentation. Although it presents these timeless songs in a new light, most of them exist in other versions on other Eva albums, the sole exception being 'San Francisco Bay Blues' which appears here for the first time.

'Songbird' was recorded live in the studio. Like many of the songs on the record, this intimate, stripped-down version effectively showcases Eva's guitar technique and her voice. Eva was quite content with the original version, on which she added the synthesizer string chords herself, but the simplicity of this acoustic version, which removes the artificial strings and the strange rhythmic click, makes the track less cloying and therefore superior.

'Wayfaring Stranger' is a real surprise since it is very different from those renditions included on *Eva By Heart* and *Songbird*. Recounting the story of a plaintive soul on a journey through life, full of trials and tribulations, who arrives home and is reunited with loved ones, the folk-style version included on this album doesn't really improve on other takes but definitely deserves to be heard. Eva's finger-picking on the opening bars is particularly strong.

'People Get Ready', a live studio recording, is another folk-style arrangement. It is a difficult song to perform solo, but Eva's voice gives it plenty of energy although the guitar part sounds uninspiring. 'True Colors', recorded live in the studio, again benefits from Eva's skilled finger-picking, which improves on the strummed chords in earlier renderings.

The version of Sandy Denny's 'Who Knows Where The Time Goes?' included here was recorded at Pearl's. A previous take recorded at the Maryland Inn with the whole band had appeared on Eva's third posthumous album *Imagine*, but without the band behind her the song sounds a bit featherless.

Of more import is the *Simply Eva* version of 'Over The Rainbow' that appeared in the Blues Alley footage which triggered Eva's rise to the top of the British charts in March 2001. This mature vocal was recorded five years after the studio version that appeared on the *Songbird* album, and ten years later the sound quality of this rendition has been improved immensely. Though far from flawless, this nevertheless makes it all the more real and convincing.

'Kathy's Song' was also recorded live at Pearl's. This reading contains three verses not included in the studio cut that appeared on *Time After Time*. Listening to different versions of all of Eva's recordings strengthens the impression that she is at her best in these simpler, more restrained performances, where she demonstrates the importance of leaving things out. This performance reinforces that notion.

'San Francisco Bay Blues', an American folk sing penned by Jesse Fuller, is the only song to appear on the album that is not featured elsewhere in her catalogue. Another song to have been recorded live at Pearl's, the audience can be heard talking in the background, which begs the question of how important it really was for these people to speak to their friends during such a wonderful performance. In collaboration with Blix Street Records, Linda Kohler-Trott showed the footage of this particular performance on her Facebook fan page.

'Wade In The Water' was recorded live at Pearl's. Blog critic 'Fitz' wrote about this version: "There's a spiritual quality to her singing that makes even an agnostic soul think twice."

On 'Time After Time', recorded live in the studio, Eva's voice is more restrained than the version that appears on the album of the same name, but it is still beautiful, as is her guitar playing.

'Autumn Leaves' was also recorded live in the studio, unlike the *Live At Blues Alley* version which featured Lenny Williams on piano, and which also appeared on the *Songbird* album. This recording is impressive, but the reason why they chose the Blues Alley version for *Songbird* is probably because halfway through the track Eva plays the wrong guitar chord.

Blix Street's liner notes say that 'I Know You By Heart' is the only *a cappella* Eva Cassidy vocal released to date, which is inaccurate. 'Way

Beyond The Blue' was an *a cappella* song (with handclapping). This 'I Know You By Heart' is a vocal-only version of the original recording. The lyrics are hair-raisingly prophetic: "You left in autumn/ The leaves were turning/ I walk down roads of orange and gold/ I see your sweet smile/ I hear your laughter/ You're still beside me every day/ Cause I know you by heart."

Simply Eva got to number four on the UK album charts on February 13, 2011, and was certified silver and then gold later that month. Eva's music clearly continues to inspire and draw in new listeners.

Epilogue

There are many who regret that Eva Cassidy has no grave. The silver-grey angel that Hugh Cassidy sculpted from scrap metal comes closest to a memorial to this exceptional woman. The angel stands in their garden, which connects Hugh and Barbara's mansion to the shore of Chesapeake Bay, the huge white house resembling a luxurious version of the cottage by the ocean side that Eva had always dreamed about. The angel's wings unfold as if she is preparing to fly away at any moment. The damp atmosphere having corroded the iron, the layer of rust on the wings gives her an almost transient quality. Her hands are folded as if she is at prayer. She radiates ethereal grace, her head tilting slightly upwards, gazing at the distant horizon.

"She represents all that is good in this world." This quotation – which Eva added to the bottom of her portrait of Bernice, Chris Biondo's dog – summarises Eva Cassidy's own life precisely. Eva loved animals because unlike people they never let her down. In her relationships with others she was always cautious, wary of unpleasantness or confrontation. The pain of her unhappy adolescence pursued her until her dying day.

But Eva Cassidy found a way of coping with the troubled waters that flowed around her life. From misery she created beautiful things. Art became a way not only of neutralising Eva's melancholy but it brightened up her existence to the point that she was able to sing "I think to myself, what a wonderful world" and really mean it. At the end of her life she was able to look back on her flawed relationship with her father and forgive him because she knew that Hugh was a victim of his own isolated upbringing.

Eva's singing brings both hope and comfort. Her music gives listeners the strength to resign themselves to mortality, at least temporarily. The first time Eva experienced this transition was while watching Judy Garland in her dusty Kansas farmyard singing 'Over The Rainbow'. Years later Eva gave millions of others the same thing, the chance to experience this song imbued with even greater emotional depth.

Art was what made Eva's life shine. She had no interest in material things. Fifteen years after her death Eva would more than likely feel completely out of place in our mass-media technological age: money, power, fame, image – all these were of no importance to Eva. It was almost as if she knew that her life on earth would be short and that it was pointless to surround herself with worldly treasures. She felt humble, like mere stardust.

Bruce Lundvall of Blue Note deeply regretted that he hadn't signed her to his label, but it was Eva who spurned him, refusing to be pigeon-holed. Fame was a terrifying prospect and success at the expense of artistic freedom was anathema to her psyche. Eva shut the door on the vast sums of money that Norah Jones, the star who saved Blue Note, would earn in her place. Eva reached for higher goals, with an innate sense that longing for something was somehow more important than attaining it.

With one notable exception, she wrote none of her own words but those songs she chose to sing so beautifully reflected her spiritual attitude to life, love, God, nature and the universe. It's not surprising that she felt attracted to Christianity as a young girl, but as she grew older she felt that the walls of a church, whether black or white, might stifle her. She was most at ease when she could embrace her softer side in a kind of spiritual sisterhood with her closest friends.

In the 15 years since her death, Eva's songs continue to appear in feature films, her albums continue to sell in vast quantities all over the world and she is a noted influence on or favourite of a diverse selection of singers and musicians, including Amy Grant, Paul McCartney, Eric

Clapton and even Ozzy Osbourne. In this respect, her story is unique. Many documentary makers, several potential authors and a handful of screenwriters have travelled to Maryland to meet with Hugh and Barbara Cassidy, all hoping to write a screenplay based on Eva's life but so far little has come of their entreaties.

Any interview with a member of Eva's family or close friends usually begins with a question about her stature as a singer. But very quickly the tone changes to one of frustration over everything that has occurred since Eva's death. In the aftermath of her all too short life came recognition. Here was an unknown artist and gifted singer finally receiving the acknowledgement she deserved when she was alive. Chris Biondo and Eva's mother, Barbara, would get together every year at The Steamboat Landing, Eva's favourite restaurant in Annapolis, to celebrate her life. Everyone felt good about discovering jewel after jewel in the tapes of Larry Melton, Keith Grimes, Lenny Williams and Biondo. Finally Eva's unique voice would be heard by the whole world.

But those celebrations didn't last. Today, the reality is that friends, family and former band members meet only in the courtroom where they are engaged in an endless litany of slightly surreal lawsuits. The life of Eva Cassidy has become a study in contrasts: unchecked admiration for a unique talent against a sad and rather shocking soap opera that has seen former friends become bitter enemies. Maybe Eva, knowing who she was dealing with, foresaw this when she hesitated to sign a record contract. She was often heard to say, "When it comes to money, people show their true colours."

Eva's music has become the battleground in a war over royalties and recognition. On the one hand Hugh and Barbara believe their daughter was heading for a solo career as a folk singer and that The Eva Cassidy Band was holding her back. Reinforcing this is their belief that the band members are seeking to benefit from Eva's posthumous success. Chris Biondo and the band, however, not only handed over Eva's recordings to her parents in good faith and feel they have suffered as a result, but maintain that the support they gave Eva contributed substantially to the subsequent sales of her records. Dan Cassidy, whose sympathies inevitably lie in both camps, now lives in

Iceland, well clear of the problems caused by the legacy of his sister's extraordinary talent.

The Facebook fanpage that Linda Kohler-Trott set up to promote *Simply Eva* attempts against its better judgment to uphold the fairy-tale image, but the innocence of Eva's music pales in the face of such bitter wrangling, and the cracks in this all too rosy picture are plain to see. Declaring your enthusiasm for one particular album over another is tantamount to taking sides in the battle for royalties. It seems Eva was indeed a bridge over troubled water and that when the bridge collapsed the waters flooded her green valley.

Is Chris Biondo right in asserting that Eva was the best singer in the world? Yes and no. There have been more mature jazz singers than Eva, purer folk singers, more convincing gospel singers and tighter R&B singers, but no one singer mastered all these genres as well as Eva Cassidy. It's about time that those concerned decided to bury the hatchet and honour Eva as one of the most versatile, authentic and gifted singers the world has ever seen. Not because it is politically correct to say so, but because it is the truth.

EVA CASSIDY
Family Tree

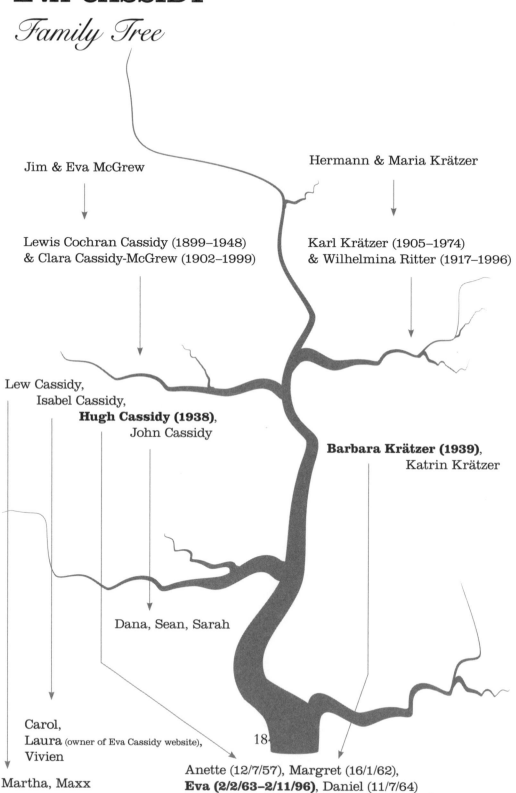

Jim & Eva McGrew

Hermann & Maria Krätzer

Lewis Cochran Cassidy (1899–1948)
& Clara Cassidy-McGrew (1902–1999)

Karl Krätzer (1905–1974)
& Wilhelmina Ritter (1917–1996)

Lew Cassidy,
Isabel Cassidy,
Hugh Cassidy (1938),
John Cassidy

Barbara Krätzer (1939),
Katrin Krätzer

Dana, Sean, Sarah

Carol,
Laura (owner of Eva Cassidy website),
Vivien

18-

Anette (12/7/57), Margret (16/1/62),
Eva (2/2/63–2/11/96), Daniel (11/7/64)

Martha, Maxx

Eva Cassidy Discography

The Other Side (with Chuck Brown), (1992) Liaison
Let The Good Times Roll (Shirley Goodman, Leonard Lee) – 3:12; Fever (Eddie Cooley, John Davenport) – 4:16; You Don't Know Me (Eddy Arnold, Cindy Walker) – 4:59; I Could Have Told You So (Jimmy van Heusen, Carl Sigman) – 3:31; Gee, Baby, Ain't I Good To You (Andy Razaf, Don Redman) – 2:44; I'll Go Crazy (James Brown) – 2:50; You Don't Know What Love Is (Gene de Paul, Don Raye) – 4:40 (Chuck Brown solo); Drown In My Own Tears (Henry Glover) – 5:37; God Bless The Child (Billie Holiday, Arthur Herzog, Jr.) – 3:18 (Eva Cassidy solo); Red Top (Ken Kynard, Lionel Hampton) – 2:55; Dark End Of The Street (Dan Penn, Chips Moman) – 3:55 (Eva Cassidy solo); The Shadow Of Your Smile (Johnny Mandel, Paul Francis Webster) – 3:30; Over The Rainbow (Harold Arlen, E.Y. Harburg) – 5:02 (Eva Cassidy solo); You've Changed (Bill Carey, Carl Fischer) – 4:00

Live At Blues Alley (1996); originally released as Eva Music (1998), both Blix Street Records
Cheek To Cheek (Irving Berlin) – 4:03; Stormy Monday (T-Bone Walker) – 5:49; Bridge Over Troubled Water (Paul Simon) – 5:33; Fine And Mellow (Billie Holiday) – 4:03; People Get Ready (Curtis Mayfield) – 3:36; Blue Skies (Irving Berlin) – 2:37; Tall Trees In Georgia (Buffy

Sainte-Marie) – 4:05; Fields Of Gold (Sting) – 4:57; Autumn Leaves (Joseph Kosma, Johnny Mercer, Jacques Prévert) – 4:57; Honeysuckle Rose (Andy Razaf, Thomas 'Fats' Waller) – 3:14; Take Me To The River (Al Green, Mabon Lewis Hodges) – 3:51; What A Wonderful World (Robert Thiele, George David Weiss) – 5:50; Oh, Had I A Golden Thread (Pete Seeger) – 4:46 (Studio recording)

Eva By Heart (1997); originally Liaison, now (1998) Blix Street Records

I Know You By Heart (Eve Nelson, Diane Scanlon) – 3:57; Time Is A Healer (Diane Scanlon, Greg Smith) – 4:14; Wayfaring Stranger (Traditional) – 4:26; Wade In The Water (Traditional) – 4:00; Blues In The Night (Harold Arlen, Johnny Mercer) – 4:05; Songbird (Christine McVie) – 3:41; Need Your Love So Bad (Little Willie John) – 4:36 (Duet With Chuck Brown); Say Goodbye (Steven M. Digman, Andrew Hernandez) – 3:55; Nightbird (Doug Macleod) – 5:27; Waly, Waly (Traditional) – 4:45; How Can I Keep From Singing? (Traditional) – 4:24

Songbird (1998) Blix Street Records / Hot Records

Fields Of Gold (Sting) 4.02; Wade In The Water (Traditional) – 4:00; Autumn Leaves (Joseph Kosma, Johnny Mercer, Jacques Prévert) – 4:41; Wayfaring Stranger (Traditional) – 4:26; Songbird (Christine McVie) – 3:41; Time Is A Healer (Diane Scanlon, Greg Smith) – 4:16; I Know You by Heart (Eve Nelson, Diane Scanlon) – 3:59; People Get Ready (Curtis Mayfield) – 3:16; Oh, Had I A Golden Thread (Pete Seeger) – 4:49; Over The Rainbow (Harold Arlen, E.Y. Harburg) – 4.57

Time After Time (2000) Blix Street Records / Hot Records

Kathy's Song (Paul Simon) – 2:47; Ain't No Sunshine (Bill Withers) – 3:26; The Letter (Wayne Carson Thompson) – 4:15; At Last (Mack Gordon, Harry Warren) – 2:58; Time After Time (Robert Andrew Hyman, Cyndi Lauper) – 4:00; Penny To My Name (Roger Henderson) – 3:41; I Wandered By A Brookside (Music: Barbara Berry/Words: Trad.

from the Alfred Williams Collection, Swindon Library) – 3:31; I Wish I Was A Single Girl Again (Harlan Howard) – 2:29; Easy Street Dream (Steve Digman) – 3:20; Anniversary Song (Steve Digman) – 2:54; Woodstock (Joni Mitchell) – 4:21; Way Beyond The Blue (Traditional) – 2:26

No Boundaries (2000) **Renata / Brunswick**

Emotional Step (Tony Taylor) – 4:50; The Waiting Is Over (David Christopher) – 3:26; You Are (Tony Taylor) – 4:56; (You Make Me Feel Like) A Natural Woman (Gerry Goffin, Carole King, Jerry Wexler) – 3:39; Little Children (David Christopher, Tony Taylor) – 3:57; I've Got This Feeling (Tony Taylor) – 4:38; When It's Too Late (David Christopher) – 4:23; On The Inside (Tony Taylor) – 4:04; Emotional Step (Radio Edit) (Tony Taylor) – 4:28; (You Make Me Feel Like) A Natural Woman (Gerry Goffin, Carole King, Jerry Wexler) – 3:33 (take 2); Little Children (David Christopher, Tony Taylor) – 3:55 (take 2)

Method Actor (2002, **reissue of 1988 LP**) **Blp**

Getting Out (David Christopher) – 4:19; Look In To My Eyes (David Christopher) – 4:16; When It's Too Late (David Christopher) – 5:00; Laugh With Me (David Christopher) – 3:43; Stay (David Christopher) – 5:24; Little Children (David Christopher, Tony Taylor) – 3:31; Forever (David Christopher) – 5:51; End The Rain (David Christopher) – 4:21; How Will It End (David Christopher, Ron Kent) – 3:38; The Waiting Is Over (David Christopher) – 3:28

Imagine (2002) **Blix Street Records / Hot Records**

It Doesn't Matter Anymore (Paul Anka) – 3:13; Fever (Eddie J. Cooley, John Davenport) – 3:57; Who Knows Where The Time Goes? (Sandy Denny) – 5:41; You've Changed (William Carey, Carl Fischer) – 4:48; Imagine (John Lennon) – 4:36; Still Not Ready (Christian R. Izzi, Leo LaSota) – 4:48; Early Morning Rain (Gordon Lightfood) – 4:05; Tennessee Waltz (Pee Wee King, Redd Stewart) – 2:33; I Can Only Be Me (Stevie Wonder) – 3:17; Danny Boy (Traditional) – 3:43

American Tune **(2003) Blix Street / Hot Records**
Drowning In The Sea Of Love (Kenneth E. Gamble, Leon Huff) – 4:19;
True Colors (Thomas F. Kelly, William E. Steinberg) – 4:50; The Water
is Wide (Traditional) – 4:21; Hallelujah I Love Him So (Ray Charles)
– 2:33; God Bless The Child (Arthur Herzog Jr., Billie Holiday) – 5:17;
Dark Eyed Molly (Archie Fisher) – 3:28; American Tune (Paul Simon) –
4:06; It Don't Mean A Thing (If It Ain't Got That Swing) (Duke Ellington,
Irving Mills) – 2:23; Yesterday (John Lennon, Paul McCartney) – 3:09;
You Take My Breath Away (Claire Hamill) – 5:39

Wonderful World **(2004) Blix Street Records / Hot Records**
What A Wonderful World (Robert Thiele, George David Weiss) – 4:20;
Kathy's Song (Paul Simon) – 2:45; Say Goodbye (Steven M. Digman,
Andrew Hernandez) – 3:56; Anniversary Song (Steven M. Digman) –
2:51; How Can I Keep From Singing? (Traditional) – 4:27; You Take
My Breath Away (Claire Hamill) – 5:40; Drowning In The Sea Of Love
(Kenneth Gamble, Leon Huff) – 4:18; Penny To My Name (Roger
Henderson) – 3:39; You've Changed (Bill Carey, Carl Fischer) – 4:47;
It Doesn't Matter Anymore (Paul Anka) – 3:13; Waly Waly (Traditional)
– 4:39

Eva Cassidy Sings **(2004, DVD) Blix Street / Hot Records**
What a Wonderful World (Robert Thiele, David Weiss) – 5:57; Cheek
To Cheek (Irving Berlin) – 3:52; People Get Ready (Curtis Mayfield)
– 3:30; You've Changed (Bill Carey / Carl Fischer) – 4:59; Time After
Time (Robert Andrew Hyman / Cyndi Lauper) – 4:04; Honeysuckle
Rose (Fats Waller / Andy Razaf) – 3:07; Autumn Leaves (Johnny Mercer
/ Joseph Kosma / Jacques Prévert) 4:44; Stormy Monday (T. Bone
Walker) – 5:43; Tall Trees In Georgia (Buffy Sainte-Marie) – 4:03; Over
the Rainbow (E.Y. Harburg / Harold Arlen) – 5:25

Somewhere **(2008) Blix Street Records / Hot Records**
Coat Of Many Colors (Dolly Parton) – 3:17; My Love Is Like A Red
Red Rose (Traditional) – 3:43; Ain't Doing Too Bad (Deadric Malone)
– 3:41; Chain Of Fools (Donald Covay) – 4:10 ; Won't Be Long (J. Leslie

McFarland) – 3:47; Walking After Midnight (Don Hecht) – 2:38; Early One Morning (Eva Cassidy, Rob Cooper) – 2:20; A Bold Young Farmer (Traditional) – 3:44; If I Give My Heart (John Pennell) – 3:59; Blue Eyes Crying In The Rain (Fred Rose) – 2:50; Summertime (George Gershwin, DuBose Heyward, Ira Gershwin) – 3:04; Somewhere (Eva Cassidy, Chris Biondo) – 4:54

Simply Eva (2011) Blix Street Records
Songbird (Christine McVie) – 2:52; Wayfaring Stranger (Traditional) – 3:07; People Get Ready (Curtis Mayfield) – 3:27; True Colors (Thomas Kelly, William E. Steinberg) – 3:47; Who Knows Where the Time Goes? (Sandy Denny) – 4:50; Over The Rainbow (Harold Arlen, E.Y. Harburg) – 5:24; Kathy's Song (Paul Simon) – 4:33; San Francisco Bay Blues (Jesse Fuller) – 3:56; Wade In The Water (Traditional) – 2:39; Time After Time (Robert Andrew Hyman, Cyndi Lauper) – 4:04; Autumn Leaves (Joseph Kosma, Johnny Mercer, Jacques Prévert) – 4:01; I Know You By Heart (a cappella) – (Eve Nelson, Diane Scanlon) – 0:54

Index